RAHENY FOOTPRINTS

Researched, written and published
by members of
Raheny Heritage Society
in conjunction with

ORIGINAL WRITING

Front Cover

Village of Raheny, 1853.

View is taken from Watermill Road, showing the bridge over the Santry River and the rath on which most of the village was built. The double bell turret of the old St. Assam's Church in the graveyard can be seen on top of the rath.

Painting by Edward McFarland.
Courtesy of the National Library of Ireland. Ref. 1986 TX (9)

Raheny Footprints

This publication features some men and women who have lived in Raheny at various times and who have, by their achievements, locally and nationally, truly left their 'Footprints in the Sands of Time'.

An Chomhairle Oidhreachta
The Heritage Council

This publication has received support from the Heritage Council under the 2009 Publication Grant Scheme

© 2009 RAHENY HERITAGE SOCIETY

978-1-907179-03-7

A CIP catalogue for this book is available from the National Library.

Published by ORIGINAL WRITING LTD., Dublin, 2009.

Printed by Cahills, Dublin.

Raheny Heritage Society was founded in January 1987 to encourage interest and research into both local and family history. The society meets regularly and holds exhibitions, outings and lectures on historical and genealogical topics. Over the years the society has assembled a large collection of old photographs and documents relating to Raheny as well as many books and magazines of general historical interest. Publications include, *Raheny Heritage Trail*, the 1901 & 1911 Census of Raheny and the 1901 Census of Clontarf East and West.

The Raheny Heritage Society would like to thank *Raheny News* and individual members of the society for their support.
The society acknowledges the help of all those, too numerous to mention, who contributed in any way to this publication. Illustrations have been individually acknowledged.

DEDICATED TO THE MEMBERS OF

RAHENY HERITAGE SOCIETY,

PAST AND PRESENT.

CONTENTS

ILLUSTRATIONS

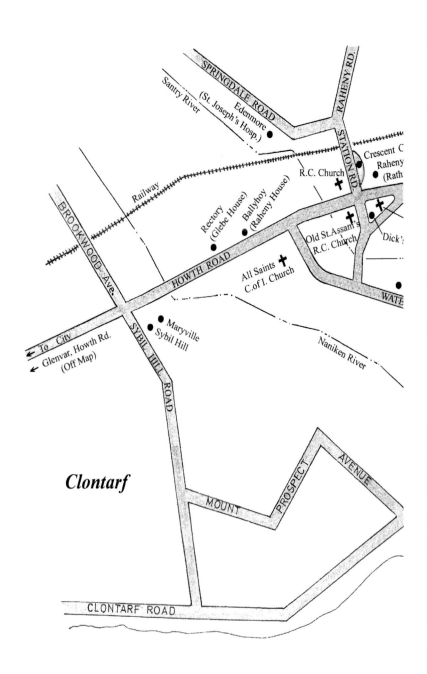

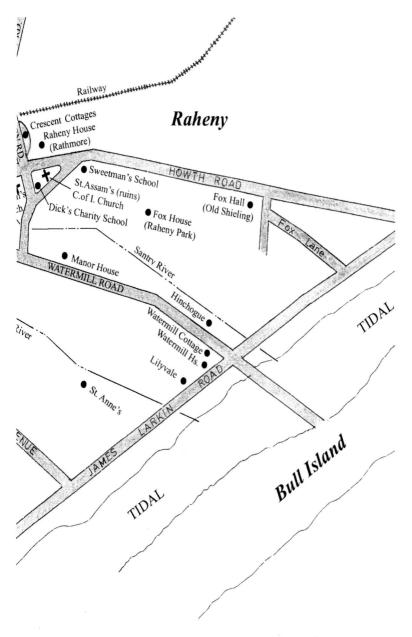

Map of Raheny

INTRODUCTION

Raheny is a modern suburb on the northside of Dublin City, close to the sea and a short commuter distance to the city centre. Formerly it was a compact rural village, surrounded by private estates, small farms and labourers' cottages. It remained largely unchanged until the spread of Dublin City began in the 1950s when new housing estates crept over the green countryside, with schools, churches and shops built to cater for the growing population. However, with its remaining eighteenth and nineteenth century houses, churches and railway station, it still retains its village atmosphere more than many suburbs of Dublin City.

The following is an extract from *A Topographical Dictionary of Ireland* by Samuel Lewis and describes Raheny in 1837.

RAHENY, a parish, in the barony of Coolock, county of Dublin, and province of Leinster, 4 1/4 miles (N. E.) from the Post-office, Dublin, on the road to Howth; containing 612 inhabitants. This place, formerly called Rathenny, derived its name from an ancient rath or moat in the centre of the village, overhanging a small stream; and is supposed to have formed part of the district called Rechen, which, together with Baelduleek (Baldoyle) and Portrahern (Portrane), was granted by Anlave, King of Dublin, to the church of the Holy Trinity, in 1040. It is also noticed under the name of Rathena, by Archdall, as the birth-place or residence of a saint about the year 570, at which time probably there may have been a religious establishment. The celebrated battle of Clontarf took place in its immediate vicinity; and it may probably have been a post of some importance, as commanding the pass of the small river which flows beneath the rath in the village.

The parish is bounded on the east by the sea: the land is in general of good quality, the greater portion is meadow and pasture, and the arable land produces excellent crops of wheat; the system of agriculture is in a very improved state, and there is neither waste land nor bog. Limestone of good quality is abundant and is quarried for building and for agricultural purposes. A constabulary police force is stationed in the village; and petty sessions are held there on alternate Thursdays. The glebe-house is a good residence, and the glebe comprises about 30 acres of profitable land. The church, a small plain edifice, is supposed to have been rebuilt about the year 1609. In the R. C. divisions the parish forms part of the union of Clontarf. About 150 children are taught in two public schools, of which the parochial school is supported by the rents of eight houses forming the crescent of Raheny, bequeathed for that purpose by the late Samuel Dick, Esq., who, in 1787, built the school-house; the R.C. school is chiefly supported by the Sweetman family, of whom the late W. Sweetman, Esq., in 1820, built the school-house, with apartments for the master, at his own expense. There is a dispensary in the village.

Samuel Dick

(1734-1802)

Linen Merchant and Banker

Samuel Dick was born circa 1734, the son of Quintin Dick of Nenagh, Co. Tipperary and his wife Anne Kerr. The Dick family settled in Dublin about 1760 and Samuel became a successful linen merchant, carrying on his business at 13 Linenhall Street, Dublin. He married Charlotte Forster on 13 November 1773 in St. Mary's Church of Ireland Parish, Dublin. Samuel came to live in Raheny in a house called Violet Hill, which dates from the first half of the eighteenth century. Mr. Dick's house is shown in 1777 on the *Taylor and Skinner's maps of the roads of Ireland*, and by 1787 Samuel had bought the property. The house was later called Edenmore House, and is now known as St. Joseph's Hospital.

Samuel Dick was a director of the Bank of Ireland for several years and Governor for the years 1797-99. He was also a director of Hibernian Insurance. By a 1789 Act of Parliament he was appointed a trustee of the Malahide Turnpike Road. He was also a member of the Ouzel Galley Society from 1772, rising in the ranks to become Captain in 1800. This society was set up in the early eighteenth century as an arbitration court by a group of businessmen, to decide the ownership of the cargo of the ship 'Ouzel Galley' which had been missing for years. After this case, they acted in a similar fashion in other cases that needed arbitration. It was the forerunner of the Dublin Chamber of Commerce. In 1789 Samuel was appointed Governor to the Hibernian Marine Society established 'for maintaining, educating and apprenticing the orphans and children of decayed seamen in His Majesty's Navy and Merchants Service'. In 1795 he was a Justice of the Peace for Dublin as well as Director of the Royal Exchange Insurance Co. of Ireland.

Portrait of Samuel Dick, Governor of the Bank of Ireland, 1797-99.
Courtesy of the Bank of Ireland.

Samuel Dick has left two important legacies in Raheny. About 1787 a new schoolhouse was built on an unused piece of the parish graveyard, in the centre of the village. It was a two-storey slated building of stone and lime with white-washed walls, reputed to have cost £150, all of which was paid by Samuel Dick. The ground floor was used as the school, with living accommodation upstairs for the schoolmaster. This school became known as 'Dick's Charity School'. The school joined the Kildare Place Society in 1828 but by 1875 most of the pupils had transferred over to the new Infant School on Station Road. Lord Ardilaun of St. Anne's acquired Dick's School in 1889 and renovated it. It was then used for some time as a Post Office and a Dispensary. Lady Ardilaun sold it in 1916 when it was known as the Village House. Over the years the building has been used for various commercial purposes. The original building was preserved when it was renovated in the late 1980s. It is the oldest building in the village.

Shortly after building the schoolhouse, about 1790, Samuel decided to build eight cottages for his workmen on his Violet Hill estate. The cottages were built in the village on a small piece of ground of 31 perches, which had previously been a potato garden. These unique Crescent Cottages, almost unchanged, still survive today and add greatly to the charm of Raheny. Samuel Dick in his will, dated 4 December 1800, left to his son, Quintin Dick and his heirs, the rent of the Crescent Cottages in trust, to pay for the salary of the schoolmaster of his Charity School. He also stated that the Master of the school should be approved by his son and heirs and if there was any surplus, it should be used to clothe 'the children of such parents as are most in want of it in the Parish of Raheny'.

Samuel Dick died on 17 January 1802 at his town house in Great George's Street, Dublin in his 69th year. According to *Jackson's Oxford Journal*, his property was estimated as being substantial. Samuel had three sons; Quintin, who became an M.P. for Malden in Essex, Hugh and William, all of whom died unmarried. His only daughter, Charlotte, married William H. Hume, M.P. for Wicklow. The eldest son, Quintin,

Main Street, Raheny in the 1950s shows Dick's Charity School, covered in ivy, facing down the street. *Raheny Heritage Society.*

Crescent Cottages, in the 1950s. Built by Samuel Dick about 1790.
Raheny Heritage Society.

carried out the conditions of the trust stated in his father's will in relation to the Crescent Cottages and the Charity School until his death in 1858. Then his sister Charlotte became responsible for the trust and as she was now living in Co. Wicklow, she transferred the trust in 1860 to Samuel Law of Kilbarrack House 'to hold for ever upon the trust of the will of Samuel Dick'. Samuel Law, a Justice of the Peace, was a governor of both Dick's Charity School and the Infant School. The legal successor to Samuel Dick's bequest today is the Board of Governors of Raheny and Coolock Schools, which still administers seven of the cottages (one has been sold).

More than anyone else, Samuel Dick has left his mark on Raheny village, which owes its distinctive and unusual character to his building of the wonderful Crescent Cottages and the old schoolhouse in the late eighteenth century.

John D'Arcy

(1787–1864)

Brewer

John D'Arcy was born in Dublin in 1787, the son of Matthew and Mary D'Arcy. He married Eliza Segrave, daughter of Peter and Jane Segrave of Ballyhoy, Howth Road, Raheny, both of whom are buried in the old St. Assam's graveyard in the centre of Raheny village. Following the deaths of the Segraves, John and Eliza D'Arcy lived in Ballyhoy from 1830 until 1864. They had four children, Matthew Peter, Jane, Mary and Eliza. The house faced the Howth Road and had a thatched roof. John D'Arcy built a new house at right angles to the old house, adjoining and retaining the thatched portion, in response to his wife's persuasion. Years later the house was called The Cottage and then Raheny House, the name by which it is still known today.

John D'Arcy had inherited a small brewery at Bridgefoot Street which adjoined the Anchor Brewery in Usher Street. The latter was owned by the Catholic Commitee leader, Edward Byrne, who settled the property on his son, John Dominic Byrne. He sold the brewery in 1818 to John D'Arcy for £35,000, which indicates the business must have been very considerable. Under D'Arcy's stewardship the business prospered and eventually the Anchor Brewery covered an area of seven acres and employed over 300 men with stabling for fifty horses. It carried on a large export trade and was second only to Guinness in capacity. In 1865 it exported 23,806 hogshead of porter (over one million gallons).

John D'Arcy was a member of Dublin Corporation for several years. He was also a Justice of the Peace and a Deputy Lieutenant of the County. In 1852 he succeeded Benjamin Lee Guinness as Lord Mayor of Dublin. The first meeting of

Portrait of John D'Arcy, Lord Mayor of Dublin, 1852.
Courtesy of the Dublin City Library and Archive.

Dublin Corporation held in the City Hall (formerly The Royal Exchange) took place on Thursday, 30 September 1852. It is recorded in the minutes of the Corporation that 'having been completed, possession of the building was publicly taken on behalf of the Corporation by the Right Honourable, the Lord Mayor, John D'Arcy Esquire, attended by the Aldermen and Councillors of the City of Dublin'. It was agreed that the building, for the future, be nominated as the City Hall.

John D'Arcy, one of the most active supporters of the Vartry Waterworks project, was one of the first members chosen to serve on the waterworks committee. He was a generous benefactor to the poor and was closely identified for many years with the Liberal Party. He worked long and zealously with Daniel O'Connell, whose friendship and esteem he enjoyed. D'Arcy was elected to the organising committee formed to build St. Assam's Catholic Church in Raheny. He subscribed £50 towards the building fund and contributed a substantial sum again shortly before his death.

John D'Arcy died at his townhouse, 15 Fitzwilliam Place on 25 February 1864, aged 77 years. His estate was valued at under £60,000. *The Freeman's Journal* of 2 March 1864 reported that at his funeral over 300 of his brewery workmen 'wearing scarves and hatbands formed four abreast at the front of the hearse, which was drawn by six horses'. It also stated that:

> notwithstanding the rain which fell heavily, crowds of the poor from the neighbourhood of Raheny and Clontarf followed on foot. The hearse bore the remains of one who was ever kind and considerate to them in their trials and necessities.

John D'Arcy was interred in the family vault in the O'Connell Circle, in Glasnevin Cemetery. It was indeed fitting that he should be buried there. Over 40 years previously in 1823, the burial of his brother, Arthur D'Arcy, in St. Kevin's churchyard in Camden Row, caused much controversy, when by order of the Protestant Archbishop of Dublin, a Catholic priest was not allowed to read the Office of the Dead at the graveside. This incident sparked off the movement, supported by Daniel O'Connell, which later resulted in the opening of Catholic cemeteries in Dublin in 1832.

Ballyhoy House, later renamed The Cottage, and now Raheny House. The original house is to the right, with the new house added by John D'Arcy on the left.
The Acorn.

JANE BARLOW

(1857–1917)

POET AND WRITER

Jane Barlow was born in Clontarf in 1857, but lived most of her life in Raheny. She was the eldest daughter of the Rev. James William Barlow, Professor of Modern History, Senior Fellow and later Vice-Provost of Trinity College. The family moved to Raheny in 1865 and lived at The Cottage, Howth Road, formerly named Ballyhoy, and now known as Raheny House.

The writer, Katherine Tynan, who was a friend of Jane Barlow, and visited her regularly, gives us an evocative description of the house. 'It was a spacious cottage, of beautiful ample living-rooms and nest-like bedrooms' and 'with a winding avenue, a wide gravel-sweep where a couple of carriages and pairs might turn without inconvenience, a beautiful old-fashion garden and all the amenities'. It had 'delicious long corridors, steps up and down into the rooms, and the Cottage had a tight-fitting cloche of thatch'. Describing the family, Katherine wrote,

> The family had lived in a practical seclusion, visiting and being visited by, I think, just the old ladies and gentlemen who lived in other secluded houses and gardens round about Raheny. I can't believe that Jane Barlow ever went to school. I think of her always in that enclosed garden of love at Raheny; but she must have been her father's pupil, for she was a good classical scholar, and in a house overflowing with books she had absorbed all that was best; she had a thoroughly cultivated mind.

Portrait of Jane Barlow by Sarah Purser.
Courtesy of Dublin City Gallery The Hugh Lane.

Jane became a popular writer of poetry and prose fiction mainly on the subject of Irish peasant life. She contributed poems and stories to a number of reviews and periodicals. She came to notice in 1892 with the publication of her first book *Bogland Studies* – a series of narrative poems in dialect, often with a strong melodramatic or pathetic story. This was soon followed by *Irish Idylls*, a work in prose, again on the theme of peasant life. She was a prolific writer and between 1892 and her death in 1917, she published an average of one volume per year. Her books, with their profusion of begorrahs, mushas and bedads may seem quaint and outdated to modern readers, but they were popular at a time when Anglo-Irish writers tended to idealise and romanticise the Irish peasant.

In 1904 Jane was conferred with an Honorary Doctorate in Literature by Trinity College - the first woman to be so honoured by the college. At the ceremony she was described as 'a woman of outstanding merit, who is exceptionally well qualified to be the first female recipient of our degree *honouris causa*'.

Jane's father died in 1913 and the following year Jane left Raheny and went to live at St. Valerie, Bray, where she died a few years later, in April 1917, aged 59 years. Her obituary in *The Times*, stated that

> every anthology of recent Irish literature includes samples of Miss Barlow's prose or verse. In her tales of Irish life she expressed both tenderness and humour, and her poetry was of a distinct quality.

Frank Gallagher

(1893-1962)

Author and Journalist

Francis David Gallagher was born in Cork City in 1893 and educated at Presentation College, Cork. He became a journalist with William O'Brien's paper, *Cork Free Press,* and was despatched to London to report on the Home Rule debates in 1914/15 from the House of Commons. In 1922 he married Cecilia Saunders from Cork, and some time later they moved to Raheny House (now the Garda Retirement Home), where they lived until the early 1930s. While there, they were visited by many well-known people, including Lady Gregory who described her visit of 3 March 1929 thus:

> Friday afternoon, a visit to the house where I had gone once to visit Jane Barlow. That house in Raheny has other tenants now – the wife gay and gentle, the husband, Frank Gallagher, proud and happy in his home and in the success of his book, *Days of Fear.* Days of peace now for both of them: their welcome very kind.... A happy peaceful hour or two.

Days of Fear was the title of Frank's hunger-strike diaries of 1919-20.

Frank joined the Sinn Féin party when he came to Dublin in 1917 and at this time he first met Eamon de Valera. With other young men who poured out of Dublin each weekend, he carried the latest policies of Sinn Féin to towns and villages to avoid the censor. On weekdays he spent most of his time at Sinn Féin headquarters, 6 Harcourt Street, preparing for the General Election of 1918.

Frank Gallagher.
Courtesy of Ann Gallagher.

Here he met Erskine Childers, for whom he developed a great admiration and they became firm friends. In the election, Sinn Féin won 73 out of 105 seats, although many of their candidates were in prison either in Ireland or England. The first Dáil Éireann met in the Mansion House, Dublin, on 21 January 1919.

During the War of Independence, Frank was first arrested in June 1919 and sentenced to four months in Mountjoy Jail for a seditious speech made in Co. Carlow. He was released in October, but in March 1920 was again interned in Mountjoy, where he partook in a mass hunger-strike of republican prisoners demanding political status. A general strike in support of the prisoners followed, paralysing the railways, trams, docks and Post Offices. The prisoners were eventually released on 14 April 1920.

Bob Brennan founded the underground newspaper, *The Irish Bulletin*, in November 1919, and Frank Gallagher, Erskine Childers and Desmond Fitzgerald were part of the production team. During the Civil War which followed the Treaty, Frank supported the Republican side and spent some time in prison during 1922/23. His wife, Cecilia, was also imprisoned and they were both in jail on their first wedding anniversary. Some time after their release, they settled in Raheny House.

When the Fianna Fáil party was formed in 1926, Frank became secretary to Eamon de Valera and accompanied him on fundraising trips to the US. De Valera intended to launch a newspaper that would reflect the views of the Fianna Fáil party, and *The Irish Press* first appeared on 5 September 1931 with Frank Gallagher as the founder editor. The 50th anniversary supplement of the paper in 1981 reproduced a letter, written by Erskine Childers to the Gallaghers the night before his execution in 1922:

Frank and Cecilia, a line of loving farewell to you two dear friends and may God bless you forever. Frank, what splendid times we have had together. You have been a great thing in my life and have given me so much. All will be well. Your faith and mine is built on rock. Goodbye to both, Erskine.

In 1935 Frank became the Deputy Director of Radio Eireann and in 1939 he was made Director of Government Information Services – a position he held throughout the war. When the Coalition Government came to power in 1948, Frank was Publicity Officer under Dr. Noel Browne in the Department of Health and in 1952 he was seconded to the Mansion House Committee on Anti-Partition. From 1954 till his death Frank was on the staff of the National Library working on preparation of a dictionary of national biography.

Frank, writing under his pseudonym 'David Hogan' contributed articles to the *Sunday Press* until his death, under the titles 'The Four Glorious Years' and 'Books from My Shelves'. The former, issued in book form in 1953, tells the story of the years 1917 - 21, including the founding of Dáil Eireann. His collections of short stories have been translated into many European languages and are included in anthologies. *The Anglo-Irish Treaty*, published after Frank's death, was a proposed biography of Eamon de Valera.

When the Gallagher family left Raheny they settled in Sutton, Co. Dublin. Frank Gallagher died on 16 July 1962. President de Valera paid tribute to his friend of over forty years, describing him as a gifted journalist, a tireless worker and a wonderful companion. Frank and his wife, Cecilia, who died in 1967, are buried in the Republican Plot in Glasnevin Cemetery.

JOHN SWEETMAN

(1752–1826)

BREWER AND UNITED IRISHMAN

John Sweetman was born in 1752 to Patrick Sweetman and his wife, Mary Sweetman who were first cousins. John was fortunate to have been born into a prosperous Catholic family of landowners and brewers, who were associated with the Raheny and Kilbarrack area from the early eighteenth century. His ancestors were enterprising farmers, some of whom turned to brewing when it came to prominence as a commercial enterprise in the early 1700s. John's father, Patrick, was the son of John Sweetman of Aston Quay brewery and his wife, Margaret Dodd. His mother, Mary was the daughter of Patrick Sweetman of Stephen's Green brewery and his wife, Mary Thunder, who lived at Fox Hall (later known as The Sheiling Hotel), on the Howth Road in Raheny. John Sweetman of the Aston Quay brewery and Patrick Sweetman of the Stephen's Green brewery and Fox Hall were brothers.

After the early deaths of his parents, John Sweetman and his elder brother, Patrick junior, were reared at Fox Hall, Raheny, by their maternal grandparents, Patrick and Mary Sweetman. When John's grandfather, Patrick, died in 1771, he and his brother Patrick became partners in the family brewery at St. Stephen's Green. John went to live at the brewery, while his brother Patrick, who married that same year, came to live in Fox House, Raheny (later named Raheny Park) which was close to Fox Hall. Their grandmother, Mary Sweetman, continued to live at Fox Hall until she died in 1784, aged 92. She is buried in Kilbarrack cemetery with her husband Patrick and daughter Catherine.

John Sweetman, United Irishman.
Elmes collection, SWET-JO(1), Courtesy of the National Library of Ireland.

In 1784 John married Mary Anne Atkinson, daughter of another brewer. John was very active in Catholic affairs in Dublin City. When the Dublin Carmelite Friars were looking for an affordable site for a church, they enlisted the help of John Sweetman. In 1792 he leased a plot of land on Clarendon Street and then sub-leased it to the Carmelites, who built St. Teresa's Church on the site. At the opening in May 1797, a memorial tablet was erected over the church entrance with an inscription in Latin, part of which read: 'John Sweetman Esquire .... laid the foundation stone of this church on 3rd October 1793.'

Besides his work in the brewery, John was actively involved with the Catholic Committee, which was set up to press for repeal of the Penal Laws. The Society of United Irishmen was founded in 1791 in Belfast and later that year in Dublin by Wolfe Tone, with the help of liberal Belfast and Dublin intellectuals, one of whom was John Sweetman. In his journals, Wolfe Tone mentioned dining at the home of his good friend, John Sweetman. Dr. R.R. Madden, in his book on the United Irishmen, described John Sweetman as:

> an eminent and opulent citizen of Dublin, of an old and highly respectable family; a man of high intelligence, sound judgment and sober, well-considered opinions, strongly attached to the rights and interests of his country.

John's brother and partner, Patrick, died in 1793 at Fox House, Raheny, aged 45 and he was buried in Swords, Co. Dublin. He left two sons, Michael (14) and Patrick (8), who came under the care of their uncle John. In 1796, the lease on the family brewery at St. Stephen's Green was running out and, mindful of the financial future of his nephews, John Sweetman acquired an established brewery at Francis Court, Francis Street. John went to live at the new brewery and many meetings of the Leinster Directory of the United Irishmen were held there. A major blow was sustained by the Society on 12 March 1798, when a raiding party arrested John Sweetman, secretary of the Leinster Directory, in the Francis Court brewery, while most of the other members of the Directory were captured in Oliver Bond's house at Bridge Street. All were charged and found guilty of treason. The prisoners were first committed to Kilmainham Jail and five months later, under the Banishment Act, twenty members, including John Sweetman, were imprisoned at Fort George, Invernessshire in Scotland. In an undated letter from Kilmainham Jail to the authorities at Dublin Castle, John Sweetman wrote of the sacrifices he had made in selling his property at two-thirds of its value to provide for his wife and two children.

Wolfe Tone died in Kilmainham Jail in November 1798 and among his effects was a pocket-book which he directed was to be sent to his old friend, John Sweetman. The green silk lining of the book was stained with blood and written in Tone's hand were the words, 'T.W. Tone Nov 11th 1798' with a quote from Virgil, translated as follows: 'now for its second master it has thee'. The pocket-book is now housed in the National Museum, Collins Barracks, Dublin.

Forbidden to return to Ireland on his release from prison in Scotland in 1802, John Sweetman, then aged fifty, was freed near Hamburg. He later settled in Paris. During this period of exile he kept in touch with his family and events in Dublin. In July 1814 the Committee for erecting a Roman Catholic Chapel in Marlborough Street advertised in Irish newspapers for designs to be submitted for the intended church. The notice was signed by John's cousin, William Sweetman of Raheny House, a trustee of the Catholic parish of St. Mary. John Sweetman is widely credited with the original design for the Pro-Cathedral, which he sent from Paris. The minutes of the Church Committee show that he was paid £307 expenses for a very large model of the church, which is still housed in the attic of the Pro-Cathedral.

John returned to Ireland in 1820 and was a member of the Pro-Cathedral building committee from September 1822 to

April 1823. After many delays, the Pro-Cathedral was opened and blessed on 14 November 1825, the feast of St. Laurence O'Toole, the diocesan patron saint. John Sweetman was too ill to attend. He died a few months later, on 23 May 1826, aged 74. He was interred in St. Columba's Cemetery, Swords in the grave in which his brother Patrick was buried in 1793.

The Francis Street brewery was run by the descendants of John's brother, Patrick Sweetman, until it was bought by the Guinness brewery in 1891. A few years later it was demolished to clear the site for the Iveagh Market which was opened in the early 1900s. Archaeological excavations in 1999 underneath the old Iveagh Market revealed part of the Sweetman brewery cellars which had been filled with rubble to make a secure foundation for the market buildings. Fox Hall, the home of his ancestors from the early 1700s, and where John was reared, was converted in 2008 into modern apartments, with only the original façade surviving.

Fox Hall where John Sweetman was reared by his grandparents, Patrick and Mary Sweetman. Later became The Shieling Hotel.
Raheny Heritage Society.

William Sweetman

(1758–1825)

Brewer and Landowner

William Sweetman (known as Billy), came to live at Raheny House, later named Rathmore, about 1810. The Sweetmans, a prominent Catholic family, had owned land and property in Raheny for several generations and Billy was a cousin of John Sweetman, the United Irishman.

In 1757, Billy's father, William, had inherited from his father, John, about 500 acres of arable land in Raheny and Kilbarrack, as well as the family brewery on Hawkins Street in Dublin City. Grain grown on the Raheny and Kilbarrack lands was used to supplement the supply of barley needed in the brewery. William Sweetman married a widow, Mary Ennis of George's Lane, on 2 February 1758. Billy was their son and on his father's death, he inherited both the brewery and the land. Billy married Jane Cosgrave in February 1781 and they had three children. Their family home was then in North Great George's Street and Billy had acquired house property around Dublin City.

In the late eighteenth century, Dublin streets were realigned by the Wide Streets Commissioners and part of the Sweetman's brewery was thus acquired about 1801. Negotiations with the Commissioners dragged on for many years and eventually Billy received over £30,000 for the whole brewery. In addition, he had a comfortable income in rents from his house properties. Now that he no longer needed to live in the city, Billy retired from brewing to live at Raheny House beside the old family possessions in Raheny and Kilbarrack. Raheny House and land was situated east of the Crescent Cottages in Raheny Village, with the entrance gates and lodge on the Howth Road, opposite the graveyard.

Raheny House, home of William Sweetman, later renamed Rathmore House.
Courtesy R. Hall.

Billy soon got involved in the life of Raheny village as dem-onstrated by the minutes of Raheny Parish Vestry in April 1820 which lists William Sweetman among thirteen people who attended. (Although he was a Catholic, as a landowner Billy was entitled to attend vestry meetings). In that same year - nine years before Catholic Emancipation – he financed the building of the first Catholic School in the village, on a site east of St. Assam's Church and graveyard and opposite the en-trance gates to Raheny House. The school had apartments for the teachers and at first it was described as 'a female School of 100 girls under the direction of Mrs. Sweetman'. Later, boys were admitted and both male and female teachers were ap-pointed. William paid the teachers' salaries until his death in 1825 and his widow continued to do so until it was designated a National School in 1835. Built of limestone at a cost of £300, with a slated roof, the school was described as a square build-ing in the 1826/27 Education Report. However, on the official application to become a National School in 1835, it measured

90 feet by 18 feet and is shown on Valuation Office maps as a T-shaped building. This suggests that the original building may have been extended. The school was in continuous use until 1875, when a new National School was erected behind St. Assam's Roman Catholic Church. In 1877 Sweetman's School was used as a dwelling house with offices. It was demolished in the 1950s and the school site was developed as shops and offices.

When Billy died in 1825, his younger son, John Andrew, inherited Raheny House and he lived there until his death in 1855. John Andrew died unmarried and his nephews, Edward Sweetman and John S. Sweetman lived in the property until 1862. In 1895 the property was acquired by the Maconchy family who changed the name to Rathmore. The house was demolished in 1960 and the many fine trees on the grounds were felled to make way for housing development.

Raheny village centre in the 1940s. Sweetman's school is the 2 storey building at far left, facing the old graveyard.
ITA collection, Courtesy of the Dublin City Library and Archive.

Thomas Michael Gresham

(1786–1871)

HOTELIER AND BUSINESSMAN

Thomas Michael Gresham lived in Dollymount, Clontarf, before he came to live in Raheny. He leased the land of Fox House, Howth Road, Raheny, from the Earl of Howth in 1835 and resided there until his death in 1871. He renovated the house and changed the name to Raheny Park. Shortly after arriving in Raheny he became active in the local Church of Ireland parish and was a churchwarden for many years. In later years he built a row of houses, on Clontarf Road, in Dollymount, called Gresham Villas.

Thomas Gresham was a foundling child, abandoned on the steps of the Royal Exchange, London and named after the founder of the Royal Exchange, Sir Thomas Gresham. It is not known when Thomas Gresham came to Ireland but he obtained employment in the service of William Beauman of Rutland (now Parnell) Square, Dublin and became butler to this family. This position was more like a secretary or manager in Irish society at that time. By 1817 Thomas was in a position to lease 21 and 22 Upper Sackville Street (now O'Connell Street, formerly called The Mall), where he opened a hotel. In 1820 he expanded the business by leasing the adjacent property, Number 20, to form an imposing frontage. He leased more property in 1824 on the west side of Sackville Street. How Thomas secured the capital to finance his business interests is not known, but it is possible he may have inherited a legacy. Gresham's Hotel became one of Ireland's best known hotels and is still in business today as The Gresham Hotel.

Over the years Thomas built and leased Gresham Terrace, Kingstown (Dun Laoghaire) and also leased property in Simmons Court, Donnybrook, Stillorgan, Dolphin's Barn, Dunsink

Gresham's Hotel c. 1820.
Leporello album, Courtesy of the Dublin City Library and Archive.

and Marlborough Street. Subsequently he became President of the Board of the Agricultural Bank, The Cholera Orphan Society and a member of The Sick and Indigent Roomkeepers' Association. In 1835 he was able to mortgage estates in England. At times Thomas had an address at The Clarence Club, Waterloo Road, London, was proprietor of Morley's Hotel, Trafalgar Square, London and also had an interest in The Royal Hotel, Kingstown (Dun Laoghaire).

A controversy in which Thomas was involved was the opposition of the residents of Kingstown to the opening of a railway, as they felt that property in the area could be devalued. Thomas was totally opposed to this project and succeeding in having the Bill in Parliament amended so that the railway ended at the West Pier which was some distance from the town centre. Later the line was extended and a new station built closer to the town. In St. John Joyce's *The Neighbourhood of Dublin* it states 'Mr. Gresham, of hotel fame, was presented with an address and 500 sovereigns, in recognition of his valiant defence of their town against the attempted invasion of the Railway although the railway was built'.

Thomas retired from the hotel business in 1865. He sold the hotel to a company, of which most of the directors were based in Cork. Thomas died on 8 May 1871 aged 84 at 8 Merrion Square, Dublin and was buried in Mount Jerome Cemetery, Dublin. His wife was Harriet Elizabeth Dearl and they had the following known children: Jonathan, Thomas Michael junior, Thomas, George Alexander, Elizabeth and Emily. His obituary in *The Freeman's Journal* stated:

There did not live a more humane and truly charitable man than Mr. Gresham, ever ready to help the poor and needy and he was always to be found amongst the most munificent supporters of the benevolent institutions of the city.

Fox House, renamed Raheny Park in 1835 by Thomas Gresham.
Raheny Heritage Society.

Stephen Lucius Gwynn

(1864–1950)

WRITER AND NATIONALIST

> The quaint arrangement of an oval wall into which the
> house was set, so that the long curves of mellow brick-
> work enclosing that acre of sunny northward sloping
> ground sprang from either hand as you looked out of the
> window.

This was how Stephen Gwynn, in his book of essays, *For
Second Reading,* published in 1918, described Raheny Park
where he lived from 1905 to 1910.

Stephen Gwynn was born in 1864 at St Columba's College,
Rathfarnham, Dublin, where his father, a Church of Ireland
clergyman, was warden. On his mother's side he was the grandson of William Smith O'Brien, the Young Ireland leader. Educated at St Columba's and at Oxford University he taught for
some years before starting as an author in London in 1896.

The cause of Ireland interested him. He joined the Gaelic League and also became involved in the opposition to the
South African Wars. In 1904 he returned to Ireland so that his
children, who had become Roman Catholics after the conver-
sion of his wife, could have a Catholic education. He settled in
Raheny Park. In *For Second Reading* he gives a most evocative
account of his attempts at small scale farming on the ten acres
surrounding the house. He describes the harvesting of apples,
the planting of potatoes and oats, bargaining for cattle and the
annual visit of the threshing machine to the local farmers.

Gwynn became involved with the Irish Literary revival and
with Irish politics. He joined John Redmond's Irish Nationalist Party and in 1906 he was invited to stand for election in
Galway City.

Stephen Lucius Gwynn.
Poole Collection, 07496. Courtesy of The National Library of Ireland.

He had no connection with the area, but the fact that he was a Protestant Home Ruler, and an earnest supporter of the Gaelic League, made him a useful asset to the Irish Party. He was elected MP for Galway against a local Unionist, Capt. Shawe-Taylor. At this time members of Parliament received no salary or working expenses. Because of the large correspondence attached to being a Member of Parliament, the Post Office installed a private letterbox at the gate lodge to his residence. At Raheny Park he entertained many distinguished visitors, including Padraig Pearse, Roger Casement, Tom Kettle, Douglas Hyde and Eoin MacNeill. His son, Denis Rolleston Gwynn (later Professor of Modern History at University College, Cork) was one of the first pupils at Pearse's school, St. Enda's, in Rathfarnham.

Gwynn was one of the founders of the Dublin publishing house of Maunsel and Company. In 1908 he became a member of the Statutory Commission set up to found the National University of Ireland. Redmond was his hero and when World War I broke out in 1914, he sided with Redmond in the belief that the cause of Ireland could best be served on the battlefields of Europe. He later enlisted as a private although he was aged over fifty at the time, and served in France for which he was awarded a Chevalier of the Legion d'honneur. When revolutionary Ireland emerged, he wrote with sympathy and encouragement of the new Irish State.

Gwynn's literary output was prolific. He became an authority on the eighteenth century and a student of Irish history, topography, sport, legend and poetry. His books include works on Tennyson, Robert Emmet, Henry Grattan, Sir Walter Scott, Dean Swift, Oliver Goldsmith, R. L. Stevenson and John Redmond. He also wrote on France and on fishing. His autobiography *Experiences of a Literary Man* was published in 1926.

He returned to London in 1923 and spent his time writing, as well as becoming a political correspondent for *The Observer* and *The Times* newspapers. He was later awarded honorary Degrees from the National University of Ireland and the University of Dublin, Trinity College, and also received the

Gregory Medal of the Irish Academy of Letters. He spent his last years in Ireland and died on 11 June 1950 in Dublin. He was buried in Tallaght cemetery. In an obituary in the *Irish Press* he was described as 'one of those men whose very entrance into a room seemed to endow it with an atmosphere of culture.'

George Papworth

(1781-1855)

George Papworth lived from 1830 until his death in 1855 in a house named Hinchogue on Watermill Road, a short distance from the coast road. This house was previously known as Bettyville Cottage and described by John D'Alton in his *History of the County of Dublin* as a 'cottage ornée'. There was a very interesting stone, dated 1572, which bore the arms of the Howth and Plunkett families, built into an angle of the house. Francis E. Ball, in his book *Howth and its Owners*, states that the house built in Raheny in 1572 by Christopher 'the blind Lord of Howth' was known as St. Lawrence's Hall by the Howth family. The house was demolished in 1910 when the tablet was removed to Howth Castle and then re-erected in an alcove on the wall of the loggia in the Castle.

George Papworth was born in London on 9 May 1781, son of English stuccoist, John Papworth (1750-1799). In 1796, when George was barely fifteen, he exhibited a design for a bath at the Royal Academy. Following his father's death, he became the pupil of his elder brother, the architect John Buonarotti Papworth, and acted as his clerk of works until 1804, exhibiting three further designs at the Academy.

In May 1806, George Papworth moved to Dublin to take charge of Circular Stone Manufacturers of North Strand, a company that operated a patented system for producing stone tubes for pipes and other uses. He also started to build up his architectural practice and refused an offer to work for other architects. George became a Freeman of Dublin in 1810 as a member of the Bricklayers' Guild. In 1808 he married Margaret Davies and they had a number of children, including John Thomas Papworth who was his assistant for a while, but

Wax relief of George Papworth by Christopher Moore.
Courtesy of the National Museum of Ireland.

predeceased him, dying in France in 1841, aged 26. His son, Collins Edgar Papworth, emigrated to Melbourne, where he worked as an engineer for the Colonial Office, while another son, Charles William Papworth succeeded him in his architectural practice after his death.

King's Bridge, designed by Papworth to commerorate the visit of George IV in 1821. Later renamed Sean Heuston Bridge and now used solely for the Luas tramline.
N. Mc Devitt.

In 1837 Papworth was appointed architect to the Ecclesiastical Commissioners for the province of Connaught, a post he held until 1842. While there he designed many churches and residences. He was also architect to the Dublin & Drogheda Railway Company and to the Royal Bank. He played an active role in the affairs of the Royal Hibernian Academy of which he was appointed Professor of Architecture. Among his designs are the King's Bridge (now Sean Heuston Bridge) built in 1827/28 to commemorate the visit of George IV to Ireland in 1821. Other works in Dublin include the Carmelite Church in Whitefriar Street and the Baptist Chapel in Lower Abbey Street. He was the architect in charge of finishing the interior of St. Mary's Pro-Cathedral from 1823 to 1827 and he also designed Kenure House, Rush, Co Dublin. Other buildings credited to him include the Royal Bank in Foster Place, Dublin (now Allied Irish Bank), the Drogheda Railway Station, Co. Louth, Balbriggan Railway Station, Co. Dublin and Middleton Park House, Co Westmeath.

George Papworth died on 14 March 1855 in Dublin and was buried in Mount Jerome Cemetery. His obituary in *The Builder* described him as a congenial companion as well as an able and inventive architect. It recorded that he had

> great skill as a draughtsman and colourist, he combined a knowledge of the means of producing effect in his executed works, as well as economy of material, and was extremely original in his methods of construction.

Grecian style Baptist Chapel, Lower Abbey Street, Dublin, designed by Papworth and opened in 1839.
J. Sharkey.

WILLIAM DARGAN

(1799–1867)

RAILWAY MAGNATE

Only part of a red-brick wall remains on the edge of St. Anne's Park near Sybil Hill to remind us of Maryville House, which stood on the site. This was the home for a few years in the early 1850s of William Dargan, one of the greatest entrepreneurs of ninteenth century Ireland.

William was born 28 February 1799 in Co. Carlow, the son of a farmer. He trained as a surveyor and secured a position in 1820 as an overseer with Telford, the great English railway engineer, who was then constructing the London to Holyhead Road. When that work was finished, Dargan returned to Ireland and became a contractor and worked on the construction of the road from Dublin to Howth, via Raheny. In fact the Howth Road was, for postal purposes, regarded as a continuation of the Holyhead to London Road and both were sometimes referred to as 'the Dublin and London Road'. The granite milestones, which still remain on the Howth Road, are the same as those at Holyhead.

In 1831 William Dargan became the contractor for the first railway to be built in Ireland, the Dublin-Kingstown line, which opened in 1834. After that he built the Ulster Canal between Lough Erne and Belfast. In fact, Queen's Island in Belfast Lough was originally known as Dargan's Island. In 1841 he was awarded the contract for the Donabate to Balbriggan section of the Dublin to Drogheda railway. Other great works that followed were the Great Southern and Western and the Midland Great Western lines. By 1853 he had constructed over 600 miles of railway and he had contracts for 200 miles more. He paid the highest wages with the greatest punctuality, and his generosity was such that he was known as the 'man with

William Dargan.
R 12663. Courtesy of the National Library of Ireland.

his hand in his pocket'. A special saloon railway car for the use of Willam Dargan was built in 1844 and is now preserved in the Ulster Transport Museum near Belfast.

In 1853 he organised the great Dublin Industrial Exhibition, mostly at his own expense. Before it was opened on 12 May 1853, his advances reached nearly £100,000, of which he ultimately lost £20,000. The Exhibition was a huge success, attracting visitors from far and wide. Queen Victoria and Prince Albert attended the Exhibition on the morning of 30 August and in the afternoon visited William Dargan and his wife at their family home in Mount Anville, Dundrum, Co. Dublin. The Queen offered Dargan a baronetcy which he declined. The works of art shown at the Exhibition formed the nucleus for the opening of the National Gallery of Ireland in 1864, in the grounds of which a bronze statue of William Dargan, sculptured by Thomas Farrell, was also erected.

Farming and flax growing were among Dargan's other interests. He rented 2,000 acres in Co. Cork on which he grew flax and he owned a linen-thread mill at Chapelizod, Co. Dublin. At the Paris Exhibition in 1855, he won a medal for flax thread. While he lived at Maryville, Raheny, he tried new ideas on scientific farming and grew sugar beet. He raised prize-winning sheep and cattle at his Mount Anville property in south Co. Dublin. He was also High Sheriff and Deputy-Lieutenant of Dublin City, and a member of the Dublin Chamber of Commerce, and of the Ouzel Galley. In later years he devoted himself chiefly to the working and extension of the Dublin, Wicklow and Wexford Railway, of which he was chairman.

In 1866 William Dargan was seriously injured by a fall from his horse and while incapacitated, his affairs became disordered, which led to financial difficulties and affected his health and spirits. He died at his residence in Fitzwilliam Square on 7 February 1867 and was buried in Glasnevin Cemetery. The mourning for him was universal and genuine; hundreds of railway workers marched in the funeral cortege and newspapers and public bodies paid tribute to a great Irishman. The *Freeman's Journal* described the death of Dargan, thus

In him Ireland has lost one of her foremost men – industry one of her ablest chiefs – the sons of toil one of their best instructors and examples.

The Times recorded that

the nature of the works which he achieved, will ensure him to stand alone as a leader of industrial progress in the history of Ireland.

The present Luas Green line tram system in Dublin incorporated part of the old Harcourt Street railway line which Dargan had built. In July 2004, an award winning cable-stay bridge was opened on the Luas line at Dundrum, near Taney Junction and named 'William Dargan Bridge' to commemorate Ireland's greatest railway engineer.

Maryville House where William Dargan lived in 1850s.
Raheny Heritage Society.

RICHARD KELLY

(1794–1866)

BUSINESSMAN

Richard Kelly lived at Manor House, Watermill Road, Raheny from June 1848 until his death in December 1866. His son, William Kelly with his family, continued to live in the house until 1904. The original house on this site was built by the Howth family in the later part of the seventeenth century and re-fronted in red brick circa 1750. It was known as Bettyville House but later was renamed Manor House and the Dowager Lady Howth lived here from 1835 to 1840.

Richard Kelly was a gun powder merchant, whose business was at 56 Lower Sackville (later O'Connell) Street. Richard was a widower with three young children, when he married on 21 October 1829, Catherine Lee, sister of Daniel Lee, a prominent merchant and ardent O'Connellite who lived in Manchester, England. Both Richard Kelly and Daniel Lee belonged to the wealthy merchant class that rendered signal service to the Catholic Church following emancipation. Richard Kelly was also a personal friend of Daniel O'Connell and was well connected to and a confidant of leading figures in the Catholic Church at the time. These include Dr Murray, Archbishop of Dublin, his successor, Dr. Cullen, Dr McHale, Archbishop of Tuam and many others. The laying of the foundation stone in 1848 of the Church attached to All Hallows Seminary in Drumcondra, was performed by Richard Kelly, who also contributed to the building fund.

Richard was a member of the '82 Club, founded in 1845, in memory of the Volunteers of 1782 and the Independent Parliament of 1792. Richard also was a member of the Loyal National Repeal Association and frequently presided at their meetings in Conciliation Hall, Burgh Quay. Richard was elected a Town Councillor as a Repeal candidate for the Post-Office Ward of

Manor House, home to the Kelly family from 1848 to 1904.
ITA collection. Courtesy of the Dublin City Library and Archive.

Dublin Corporation in 1845 which he served for many years. He was also a Justice of the Peace and declined the position of Chief Magistrate. He was an active member of the Poor Law Board, the Dublin Hospital Board of Superintendents and many other charitable institutions.

Monsignor Fitzpatrick, PP Raheny, writing in the *Acorn* magazine in 1963, stated that there were very close relationships between the Kelly family and the Catholic hierarchy in Ireland and Rome. He wrote

In 1847 Richard and his eldest son Peirse went to Rome, where they had an audience with Pius IX and were received at the Irish College by Dr Kirby, its president. When Dr Cullen, Archbishop of Armagh was transferred to Dublin in 1852, the Papal Bulls were sent through Dr. Kirby to Richard Kelly for personal delivery and were placed in the hands of the Archbishop by Peirse Kelly.

Wedding in August 1953 at St. Assam's Catholic Church showing
the Kelly Memorial Window over the altar.
Courtesy of the O'Connor family.

The recent release of the papers of Dr. Kirby and Dr. Cullen, held in the Pontifical Irish College in Rome, appears to confirm this sequence of events. A few years later in 1856, Archbishop Cullen performed the ceremony at the marriage of Richard's younger son, William.

Richard Kelly was an uncle of William Howard Russell, who worked for *The Times* in London and became famous as a war correspondent, after he spent 22 months covering the Crimean War including the Charge of the Light Brigade. In 1855 Russell came to Dublin to receive an Honorary Degree at Trinity College and afterwards he went to dine with his uncle at Manor House.

When in 1859 it was proposed to build a Catholic church in Raheny - the first for three hundred years – Richard Kelly was a member of the Church Building Committee. The subscription list included Richard and his son, Peirse Kelly and was headed by Richard's brother-in-law, Daniel Lee who donated £100. This church, dedicated to St. Assam, was opened in 1864 by the Archbishop of Dublin, Dr Cullen. Two years later, on Christmas Day 1866, Richard died at Manor House and he was buried in Glasnevin cemetery near Daniel O'Connell's grave. His obituary in the *Freeman's Journal* described him as 'a kind parent, a good citizen, and a generous-hearted friend' and stated that 'his memory will long live in the minds of those who knew his public worth'.

In 1869 a tripartite stained glass window was erected in the east window over the altar in the new St. Assam's Catholic Church. It was a memorial window to Richard Kelly and his wife, Catherine, and was paid for by Daniel Lee. The inscription, at the base of the window, reads as follows:

Of your charity pray for the repose of the souls of Richard Kelly, T.C. J.P. of Manor House, Raheny, who died 25th December 1866 and of Catherine, his wife, who departed to Our Lord on 6th November 1867.

Details of Kelly Memorial window, depicting St. Bridget,
Our Lord and St. Patrick, with inscription underneath.
The Acorn, Mar-Apr, 1963.

Pray also for the good estate of Daniel Lee of Manchester, who has caused this window to be erected to the memory of his dear sister and brother-in-law, and of Frances Elizabeth F. Lee, his wife and their children. AD 1869.

Richard Kelly was survived by three children: Peirse, who was the Crown Solicitor for Waterford, William who worked in the family business in the city and a daughter, Ellen. William continued to live at Manor House and for years was a familiar sight, even in old age, passing through the village every day to the station to catch his train to town. His death in 1904 marked the end of the Kelly connection with the Manor House in Raheny.

BENJAMIN LEE GUINNESS

(1798–1868)

BREWER AND PHILANTHROPIST

Benjamin Lee Guinness, born on 1 November 1798 in Dublin, was the grandson of the first Arthur Guinness who founded the St. James's Gate brewery in 1759. He started working in the brewery at the age of sixteen alongside his father, Arthur II, becoming the controlling partner from 1838 onwards and head of the brewery after his father's death in 1855.

In 1835 Benjamin Lee and his brother, Arthur Lee came to live in Clontarf when they acquired a small estate with 50 acres, called Thornhill, from John E.V. Vernon of Clontarf Castle. The Thornhill estate was situated in the townland known as Blackbush or Heronstown, in the civil parish of Clontarf. It had a splendid situation: beside the sea, on a natural height, overlooking Dublin Bay, with views stretching from Howth Head to the Dublin and Wicklow Mountains. The Naniken River was the northern boundary of the property, and was also the boundary between the civil parishes of Clontarf and Raheny. Within a few months of moving into Thornhill, the Guinness brothers added to the estate by acquiring adjoining land in Raheny. In 1837 Benjamin Lee married his first cousin, Elizabeth Guinness, and built an impressive and luxurious new house for himself and his wife. This new house, called St. Anne's, after the nearby holy well on the Raheny side of the estate, was built by 1837 and incorporated part of the Thornhill house. It was an irregular shaped Italian style house, with an unusual observation tower on the roof, which was a replica of the Roman Tomb of the Julii at St. Rémy in France.

In January 1838, Arthur Lee sold his share of St. Anne's to his brother, Benjamin Lee, withdrew from the brewery partnership and went to live in Stillorgan Park. The St. James's

Benjamin Lee Guinness. *Drawing by W.A. Wragg,
Courtesy of the National Library of Ireland.*

Gate brewery expanded and flourished under Benjamin Lee's control and his increased wealth was lavished on his St. Anne's estate. In 1839 he built an ornamental tower bridge over the entrance drive from the coast road on the estate to mark the occasion of the birth of his first child, a daughter, named Anne Lee. Three sons were later born: Arthur Edward, born in 1840; Benjamin Lee, in 1842; and Edward Cecil, in 1847. Over the years, the amount of land on the Raheny side of the estate was reduced but at the same time Benjamin Lee acquired another small estate and house, called Bedford Lodge on the Clontarf side. By 1855 the total area of St. Anne's estate was around 85 acres, i.e. 62 acres in Clontarf and 23 acres in Raheny.

Both the house and the landscaping of the gardens reflected Benjamin Lee's interest in Italian architecture and design. A formal walled garden was laid out and made into 'an outdoor sculpture gallery for a collection of marble statuary' bought by Benjamin Lee on his travels in Italy, with a background of castellated yew hedges. A water-temple, based on a Pompeian model, was erected on the artificial lake formed by damming the Naniken river and a Herculanean temple was also built overlooking the river. A walled vegetable garden was built with an entrance through gates under a four-storey brick clock tower, which had a giant bell, inscribed with Benjamin Lee's name and the family motto *Spes Mea in Deo* (My Hope is in God). At a later stage, a large conservatory was added to the east side of the house.

Benjamin Lee was deeply religious: he respected his wealth and felt it was a sacred trust to be used for the good of others. He also took an active part in the local parish life of the Church of Ireland in Raheny and was a trustee of the Raheny Infant School, on Station Road, which he served until his death. In 1839 he proposed to build a new church for Raheny parish but this never happened as obviously no suitable land became available. Years later, it was his son, Arthur Edward who fulfilled his wish.

Benjamin Lee became the most prominent and successful figure in Irish business life. With his increased wealth he was able to buy, in 1852, the Ashford estate in Cong, Co. Mayo along with large tracts of land stretching from the shores of Lough Corrib to Lough Mask. He created employment for the area with his additions to the house and improvements to the estate as well as road building and land reclamation. He next acquired a substantial town house in Dublin when he bought 80 St. Stephen's Green in 1856. Then he bought the adjoining property and converted the two into one house with a unified façade of Portland stone, acting as architect himself to the remodelling. From then on it became the Guinness family's town house, establishing a splendid tradition of entertaining for three generations of brewers. His grandson, the second Earl of Iveagh, donated the house to the nation in 1939 when it was renamed Iveagh House and became the headquarters of the Department of Foreign Affairs.

Benjamin Lee was elected Lord Mayor of Dublin in 1851 and was a Conservative and Unionist Member of Parliament for Dublin from 1865 to 1868. He was a major contributor to the Dublin Exhibition of Arts and Industries in 1865. His greatest act of generosity to his native city was his restoration of St. Patrick's Cathedral, which he saved from falling into ruin. The restoration cost him personally almost £150,000 and took several years to complete. He also financed restoration of the nearby Marsh's Library and the layout of a new approach road. He was created a baronet in 1867 and this was the first title to be bestowed on a member of the Guinness family. He did not live long to enjoy it, as he died suddenly the following year in 1868 in London. His remains were brought back to St. Anne's and lay there for six days in his private chapel, which was described by the *Freeman's Journal* as 'a gem of neatness and grandeur'. His funeral cortege from St. Anne's to interment at Mount Jerome Cemetery was an impressive demonstration of public sorrow, with over 500 carriages and a thousand working men, walking four deep, covering a length of two miles. After his death, in recognition of his generous support to St. Patrick's Cathedral, a statue by the sculptor, John Henry Foley was erected in the grounds.

Clock Tower, St. Anne's, built by Benjamin Lee Guinness in 1850.
Courtesy of D. McIntyre.

At the time of Benjamin Lee's death, St. James's Gate brewery was the biggest porter brewery in the world. He left an estate valued at one million pounds, making it the largest will proved in Ireland up to that date. The brewery was left equally between his eldest son, Arthur Edward, and his youngest son, Edward Cecil. St. Anne's estate was inherited by his eldest son, Arthur Edward.

Arthur Edward Guinness

Lord Ardilaun

(1840–1915)

BREWER AND PHILANTHROPIST

Arthur Edward Guinness, the eldest son of Sir Benjamin Lee Guinness, was born on 1 November 1840 at St. Anne's. He was educated at Eton and obtained an MA degree from Trinity College, Dublin in 1866. On his father's death in 1868, he inherited his baronetcy and his parliamentary seat. He also inherited the two estates of St. Anne's in Dublin and Ashford in Co. Galway. The Guinness town house in Stephen's Green was left to his youngest brother, Edward Cecil, with the brewery business left equally between the brothers, Arthur Edward and Edward Cecil.

On 16 February 1871 Arthur Edward married Lady Olive Charlotte White, the daughter of William, third Earl of Bantry. The couple settled in St. Anne's and later acquired a town house at 18 Leeson Street, Dublin. Following Gladstone's Irish Church Act which disestablished the Church of Ireland, Sir Arthur proposed in December 1872 to contribute to the endowment of Raheny parish, and in return, he wanted the future right of presentation of a rector to himself and his heirs. The parishioners gratefully accepted his proposal and Sir Arthur nominated the Reverend Francis Hayes as rector of Raheny parish, where he served for over 40 years.

The major expansion and development of St. Anne's estate was due mainly to Sir Arthur Guinness and his wife Olive. The land was acquired over a relatively short four-year period, from 1874 up to 1878. Sir Arthur paid a total of £18,000 in June 1874 to the Earl of Howth for the lease of 277 acres of

Arthur Edward Guinness, Lord Ardilaun.
Courtesy of the Royal Horticultural Society.

Raheny land. He then acquired two other nearby estates, Sybil Hill and Maryville, which brought the total area of St. Anne's estate to slightly under 500 acres. In 1873, he commissioned the architect, James Franklin Fuller, to plan and supervise the remodelling of his house at St Anne's, almost doubling it in size, with Thomas Millard as builder. It took about seven years to complete. Apparently Sir Arthur and Fuller had a disagreement, and another architect, George Coppinger Ashlin, was entrusted with completing the house. It was described as the 'most palatial house built in Ireland during the second half of the 19th century'. One of the most interesting new features was a winter garden in the centre of the mansion, called a palm court, with a glass roof. It adjoined the main hall and upper gallery, and measured 66 feet by 38 feet (21.1 metres by 11. 5 metres). It was during this remodelling that the Roman tower erected by his father on the roof of the house was removed and resited on a mound overlooking the lake, where it still stands today.

St. Anne's House, front view at a garden party in 1912.
Gillman collection, Irish Architectural Archive.

Sir Arthur continued to be a partner with his brother Edward Cecil in the brewery, but over the years, he showed a declining interest in the active management of the business. On 12 October 1876, the partnership was finally dissolved on very favourable terms. Sir Arthur was now a very rich man and this retirement sum, together with his many other investments, left him free for his real interests, public life and philanthropy. A general election had been called in 1874, and Sir Arthur again stood as a Conservative and Unionist candidate for Parliament and regained his seat, which he had lost in 1869.

Sir Arthur and Lady Olive were greatly influenced by French houses and gardens, and this was seen at St Anne's when they laid out grand *allées* radiating from the house. A new main avenue was laid out westwards from the house, which ran in a straight line one mile long and was flanked on either side by alternative plantings of the evergreen Holm Oak and Austrian Pine. The new avenue caused a problem for Sir Arthur as it cut across a by-road called Wade's Lane, which was a short cut for Raheny people to get to Clontarf, and local people were still entitled to use this 'right-of-way'. He overcame this problem and preserved his privacy by constructing a tunnel under the main avenue. This facilitated local people, while also preventing them being seen by him as they crossed the main avenue of his estate.

Sir Arthur also found time to spend his money on many other projects in Dublin. Along with his brother, Edward Cecil, he funded the Dublin Exhibition in 1872. He continued the work his father had commenced on reconstructing Archbishop Marsh's Library near St Patrick's Cathedral, while also clearing slums in that area. He rebuilt the Coombe Lying-in Hospital and served for 16 years as President of the Royal Dublin Society. He was also President of the Royal Horticultural Society from 1894 onwards. His biggest project was acquiring the then private park of St Stephen's Green from all the keyholders, personally spending £20,000 on landscaping the park with walks, flowerbeds and an ornamental lake, and then opening it as a public park on 27 July 1880. His many acts of generosity to his native city were rewarded when he was raised to the peerage and took his seat in the House of Lords. He took the name, Ardilaun, *ard oileán*, meaning 'high island', after the name of the island in Lough Corrib on his Ashford estate. This was the first peerage to be bestowed on a member of the Guinness family. In 1892, Dublin Corporation erected a statue of Lord Ardilaun, by the sculptor Thomas Farrell, in St Stephen's Green, as a token of appreciation for his munificence to his native city.

Lord Ardilaun also spent a vast amount of money turning his Ashford estate in Galway/Mayo into a massive baronial castle with many practical improvements to the estate and surrounding area. He bought the Muckross estate in Kerry, which included the Lakes of Killarney, in 1899 for £60,000, to save it from commercial development.

Sir Arthur took an active interest in the parish of Raheny. When the Parochial School and Crescent Cottages, built by Samuel Dick in late eighteenth century, were in need of repair, he paid for their renovations. As a trustee to the Raheny Infant School he was a major contributor to the building of the new school on Station Road in 1875. His lasting legacy to Raheny was the building of a new church for the parish, in 1889, at his own expense, on a site in St Anne's estate, to replace the old church of St Assam. It was designed by George Ashlin, who was finishing the remodelling of the St. Anne's mansion, and was built by Messrs Collen Brothers of Dublin and Portadown. It has been described as a 'gem of Irish architecture'. The new church was called All Saints', in memory of his father, Sir Benjamin Lee, who was born on All Saints' Day, 1 November, as also was Lord Ardilaun himself. The same architect and contractors, also built new red brick stables for Lord Ardilaun on a site near his mansion, known today as the Red Stables, which are enclosed within iron gates and railings.

Lord Ardilaun died on 20 January 1915 at St Anne's and his widow lived on at St. Anne's until her death in 1925. Both are buried in the mortuary chapel in All Saints' Church. As they had no children the estate passed to Lord Ardilaun's nephew, Bishop Plunket, who lived there for ten years but then sold it

All Saints' Church, Raheny, built by Lord Ardilaun and opened in 1889.
J. Sharkey.

to Dublin Corporation in 1938. The mansion was accidentally burned down in 1943 and finally demolished in 1968. Part of St. Anne's estate was developed for both private and tenant purchase houses in the 1950s. Most of the landscaped land developed over the years by the Ardilauns has now become the beautiful public park of St. Anne's, providing a vast recreational facility enjoyed by everyone and maintained by the Parks and Landscape Division of Dublin City Council.

Patrick Boland, snr.

(1792–1871)

Patrick Boland, jnr.

(1840–1877)

BAKERS

Patrick Boland, the son of a Kildare farmer, after working as a journeyman baker in Dublin for some years, opened his own bakery in Capel Street in 1823. The business prospered and comprised a small biscuit making plant as well as the bakery. As was the custom at that time Patrick lived over the shop, but as the business prospered, he was able by 1848 to acquire an 'out-of-town' residence at Watermill House, Raheny where Patrick and his family lived until 1872.

Watermill House was situated on the corner of Watermill Road and the coast road. The adjoining estate to Watermill House was St. Anne's estate, the home of Benjamin Lee Guinness, head of St. James's Gate brewery. Initially Patrick Boland held 13 acres of land around Watermill House but by 1855 this had increased to 38 acres. He also acquired an additional 49 acres of land nearby in Raheny South townland which had a frontage onto the Howth Road. The Earl of Howth was the owner of most of the land in Raheny and a survey of the Howth Estate in 1863 showed that all the land was used mainly for growing wheat and oats. Obviously Patrick Boland had acquired the extra land in Raheny in connection with his bakery business.

Patrick Boland was a devout Catholic and for over thirty years he taught catechism at the Pro-Cathedral. He married Elizabeth Plunkett, a Protestant, who was from Belfast, but all

Boland's Mills, Grand Canal Dock.
Courtesy of the Irish Architectural Archive.

their children were reared as Catholics. Patrick was a contributor to the building of the new St. Assam's Catholic Church in Raheny which opened in 1864. Patrick was well known for his generosity and charity and when anyone in distress asked him for help, none went away empty handed. He was also an ardent supporter of Daniel O'Connell. Patrick died at Watermill House on 12 December 1871 aged 79. His funeral from Raheny to Glasnevin Cemetery attracted large numbers and as reported in the *Freeman's Journal* 'the inhabitants of Dollymount and Clontarf closed their establishments as did also most of the residents in Capel Street'. He was buried in his family chapel and vault which he had established close to the Daniel O'Connell tower. After Patrick's death, his wife Elizabeth Boland was received into the Catholic Church, but she died a few months later on 29 November 1872. In June 1874, all the Boland lands in Raheny, as well as adjoining properties, were acquired by Sir Arthur Guinness, son of Benjamin Lee Guinness, and became part of the enlarged St. Anne's estate.

Boland Family Mausoleum, close to the Daniel O'Connell Tower,
Glasnevin Cemetery.
J. Sharkey.

Patrick and Elizabeth had eight children, six daughters and two sons, but one son died in infancy. Patrick Boland, Jnr., the only surviving son, was born 10 October 1840 in Capel Street. He had spent several years in America working in the bakery business and came back to Ireland in 1866 to take over Boland's Bakery from his father. Over the next nine years he worked at turning the business into a huge success. He acquired Ringsend Mills, then known as Pim's Mills, renamed it Boland's Mills, thus adding milling to his bakery business. He opened a second bakery in Dun Laoghaire and later another bakery in Grand Canal Street. Within a short time the Boland family became very wealthy. Patrick married Mary Anne Donnelly in 1866 and they lived for a short time in Belvidere House, Sandymount but after the death of his parents, Patrick came back to live in the Raheny area. In 1875 he took a 99 year lease on the house, Raheny Park, with its 53 acres which had an entrance on the coast road, near Watermill House, where he had lived as a child. The house also had an entrance on the Howth Road. At Raheny Park, Patrick tried experimental farming methods and also spent money on improvements to the house.

Patrick was keenly involved in the Agrarian Reform movement. It was at Raheny Park that he and Andrew Kettle founded the Tenants' Defence League, with Patrick also furnishing the offices of the League in Sackville (later O'Connell) Street, Dublin. He only lived for two years in Raheny Park as he died there on 17 May 1877, after a short illness, at the young age of 36, leaving his wife Mary with seven young children. His estate was valued at £100,000. Patrick was buried in the family vault in Glasnevin. Mary only remained for another year at Raheny Park and moved to Winton House, Leeson Street in Dublin. Mary Boland, as the widow of Patrick junior, became the legal owner of the lease of Watermill House and land. As this had now become part of St. Anne's estate, she received compensation in 1878 from Sir Arthur Guinness for the surrender of the original lease.

After Patrick's death in 1877, Mary Boland's brother Patrick Donnelly, took over the management of the Boland Bakery business. Only five years after the death of her husband, Mary Boland died in 1882 and her half brother, Bishop Nicholas Donnelly became the guardian of her seven young children. In 1888 Boland's became a public company and the prospectus for the company listed the extent of the business as follows:- Metropolitan Baker at 133-136 Capel Street, City of Dublin Bakery at Grand Canal Quay, Model Bakery at Cumberland Street and Upper George's Street, Kingstown (now Dun Laoghaire), as well as the Boland's (Ringsend) Flour Mills. There were 800 workers employed in Boland's at this time.

John Pius Boland, born in 1870, a son of Patrick and Mary Boland was educated in London, Oxford and Bonn University. In 1896 on a visit to Athens he entered the Olympic Games and won gold medals for lawn tennis in the singles and the doubles events, thus becoming Ireland's first Olympic Champion. He later became a nationalist MP for South Kerry from 1900 to 1918 and died in 1958. His daughter, Mrs. Honor Crowley continued the political tradition by becoming a Dail TD for South Kerry from 1945 to 1965. Another daughter of John Pius Boland, Bridget Boland, became a well-known playwright and author.

Boland's Mills was one of the buildings occupied during the Easter Rising in 1916. It was held by the 3rd Battalion of the Irish Volunteers, led by Eamon De Valera. It was the last building to surrender to the British Army. In 1966 a commemorative plaque was mounted into the wall at the premises at Grand Canal Street, and unveiled by the then President of Ireland, Eamon De Valera. In 1984 Boland's Mills was acquired by The Irish Agricultural Wholesale Society Ltd. (IAWS) and in 2001 production ceased and the site was sold for development.

Henry Chichester Hart

(1847-1908)

BOTANIST, EXPLORER AND PHILOLOGIST

Henry Chichester Hart, the son of Sir Andrew Searle Hart, Vice-Provost of Trinity College, was born on 29 July 1847, at Glenvar, Howth Road, Dublin. He was educated at Portora Royal School, Enniskillen, Co. Fermanagh and Trinity College Dublin. His roots were in Co. Donegal where the family had been settled since Elizabethan times. He is known primarily as a botanist, but was distinguished in three fields of activity; physical, scientific and literary.

Described as a man of 'magnificent physique' he once walked from Dublin to Lugnaquilla Mountain in Co. Wicklow and back in twenty-four hours. He was one of those who pioneered the study of plant distribution in Ireland and in 1898 he published *The Flora of County Donegal* which set a pattern for similar works. Before that, he had published other works including *The Flora of Howth* (1887) and had surveyed islands, river valleys, stretches of coastline and several mountain ranges. He had also published studies of the plants found on the Aran Islands, along the River Suir, the Galtee Mountains and mountains in Counties Mayo and Galway. A species of saxifrage, first noted by him in Co. Donegal, was featured on a stamp by An Post in 1988.

Hart also did botanical work outside Ireland: in the Arctic, Sinai and Palestine. Plants collected by him are in the British Museum and in the National Herbarium in Glasnevin, Dublin. He was a naturalist to the British Polar Expedition of 1875–1876 to the Arctic, on board *HMS Discovery,* during which he identified a new type of fungus.

Henry Chichester Hart.
Courtesy of the National Library of Ireland. Ref. 2B 594.

Hart's literary abilities were also formidable. He was an authority on the Ulster dialect, particularly that of Co. Donegal. In later years he edited some of Shakespeare's works. Hart was appointed High Sheriff for Co. Donegal in December 1894, a member of the Royal Irish Academy in 1895, and a Fellow of the Royal Geographic Society in 1898.

Hart married Edith Donnelly on 15 June 1887 in Swords, Co. Dublin and they lived in Carraghblagh, Co. Donegal as well as in Dublin City. Two children were born to the couple but the marriage ended in divorce in 1897. Hart married his second wife, Mary Cheshire in 1907. He died at his home in Donegal in 1908 and was buried at Glenalla, in a spot chosen by himself, amidst the beautiful scenery of his ancestral home.

George Derwent Thomson

Seoirse Mac Tomáis

(1903-1987)

Linguist and Classical Scholar

George Thomson, who lived at Watermill Cottage, Raheny for a short time in the 1930s, was the person who inspired Muiris Ó Súileabháin to write that great Irish classic of Blasket life, *Fiche Blian ag Fás*. He also produced, with Moya Llewelyn-Davies (who lived at Furry Park House, Killester), an English language translation of Ó Súileabháin's book, *Twenty Years A-Growing*, and it too was acclaimed a classic.

George Thomson was born at Dulwich, London in 1903 and was educated at Dulwich College and at King's College, Cambridge, where he specialised in Greek literature and early Aegean civilisation, taking a first class honours degree. His mother's family was Irish and the young George attended Irish language classes before he went to Cambridge. In fact he had wished to do Celtic Studies at college but this subject was not available. He gained a scholarship to Trinity College, Dublin where he spent a year teaching and researching and wrote his first book, *Greek Lyric Metre*. On the advice of Robin Flower, who had learned Irish in the Blaskets and whose friendship with Tomás Ó Criomhthain, the author of *An t-Oileanach,* is well known, Thomson went for the first time in 1923 to the Blaskets where he met Muiris Ó Súileabháin, then aged nineteen. Muiris recounts in his book, 'George and I spent the next six weeks walking together on strand, hill and mountain and after spending that time in my company, he had fluent Irish.' George and Muiris became close friends.

George Thomson (left) with Muiris Ó Súileabháin (right),
in civic guard uniform, c. 1928, Dublin.
Courtesy of Mrs. Maire Kavanagh.

Muiris Ó Súileabháin contemplated emigrating to Boston like so many of his family, but George prevailed on him to remain in Ireland and join the newly formed Civic Guard. One of the most fascinating episodes in *Fiche Blian ag Fás* is this young island man's journey from Dingle and his arrival in the city of Dublin. He was awe-struck at the traffic, the lights and the noise and above all at Furry Park House, which he described as 'the castle'.

Ó Súileabháin was posted to Connemara, and Thomson, by then teaching in University College, Galway, encouraged him to write his autobiography. *Fiche Blian ag Fás* was published in 1933 and its English translation by Thomson and Llewelyn-Davies appeared simultaneously in England and the U.S.A. enjoying an immediate success. The book was first offered to An Gúm, the Government publishing company, but they would only agree to publish it if references to youths drinking pints at the Ventry Races were removed, and if there was no English translation. Thomson would not agree to these conditions and published it at his own expense.

Thomson taught Greek through Irish at U.C.G. from 1931 to 1934. A story current at the time concerning his appointment to the post goes as follows:- The College authorities had decided to give the lectureship to an Irish speaking clergyman believing that this Cambridge graduate, though otherwise well qualified, would not have the necessary command of the Irish language. To their amazement Thomson spoke fluent Irish and he was appointed. As well as his published work in English, Thomson published several works in Irish including *Breith Báis ar Eagnaí* in 1929 and *Tosnú na Feallsúnachta* in 1935. He became a champion of the Irish language.

When Thomson was living at Watermill Cottage, the local Garda Sergeant, Peter O'Reilly paid him a visit that O'Reilly later recounted in the *Acorn* magazine. O'Reilly expected to meet an old, absent-minded professor with a long white beard and was pleasantly surprised to meet a young man in his early thirties who, when O'Reilly enquired about the maps on his study wall was told, 'My two greatest interests – Ireland and Greece'.

Thomson became a Fellow of his College at Cambridge and distinguished himself in the world of Greek and Homeric scholarship. He was appointed Professor of Greek at the University of Birmingham in 1937 and occupied that Chair until 1970. He published in 1938 his major edition of the *Oresteia* of Aeschylus, acknowledged by critics to be one the greatest editions of a classic work. It is dedicated to Muiris Ó Súileabháin.

In the meantime Thomson had become a committed Marxist believing that this movement was the best way forward for mankind. He published several works in which he attempted to interpret the legacy of Greece in the light of Marxism. Amongst the best known of these are *Aeschylus and Athens* (1941), *The Prehistoric Aegean* (1949) and *The First Philosophers* (1955). In the preface to *Aeschylus and Athens*, he acknowledged his debt to the Blasket islanders:

> I must also mention a special debt to my friends, the peasant fishermen of the Blasket Island in West Kerry, who taught me, among other things that could not have been learned from books, what it is like to live in a pre-capitalist society.

Thomson wrote Modern Greek and Irish with fluency and learned to read Chinese. His books have been translated into many languages. In 1979 he was honoured by the University of Thessaloniki for his services to Greek Studies and in 1976 he attended Listowel Writers' Week to mark the re-publication of *Fiche Blian ag Fás*. He continued his interest in the Blasket culture to the end of his life and one of his last works was an essay entitled 'An Blascaod Mar a Bhí' (The Blasket that was). George Thomson died in Birmingham on 3 February 1987.

Seosamh mac Grianna

(1900-1990)

WRITER

Seosamh Mac Grianna, regarded by many as the foremost Irish-language writer of Ulster and a major figure in Irish literature generally, lived for a few years in the 1950s in a cottage called Lilyvale, at the coast end of Watermill Road.

Mac Grianna, or Joe Feilimi, as he was known locally, was born at Rannafast, Co. Donegal into a talented family steeped in oral tradition. His brother, Seámus Ó Grianna, was also a writer, under the pen-name of 'Máire' and two of his other siblings were 'seanchaithe'. Seosamh was educated at St. Eunan's College in Letterkenny and St. Columb's College in Derry. He won a King's Scholarship and trained as a teacher at St. Patrick's College, Drumcondra, from where he graduated in 1921. Although Seosamh was extremely intelligent, with a passion for literature since childhood, his independent and inquiring mind found formal schooling very difficult. He described his time in St. Patrick's thus: 'It was there that I understood the pain suffered by anyone with a mind'.

He became a member of the I.R.A., took the Republican side in the Civil War and was imprisoned with his three brothers for fifteen months. From 1923 to 1927 he tried to make a living through teaching but never stayed long in any one school. Eventually he abandoned teaching to concentrate on writing. His friend and fellow Donegal man, Niall Ó Dónaill, believed that it was at this time that the strain of teaching caused Seosamh to have a nervous breakdown, which led to his mental illness in later life.

He had strong views on writing through Irish, wishing to write about contemporary Ireland with all its faults, rather than the idealised picture that was presented by many Irish writers at that time. He believed that dross should not be

Seosamh Mac Grianna.
Courtesy of the Lagan Press.

published just because it was in Irish and was greatly encouraged by reading the works of Padraig Ó Conaire, who wrote about such subjects as madness, murder and suicide. Mac Grianna contributed articles to journals including an *tUltach* and *Fáinne an Lae*, and, after 1931, to the newly launched *Irish Press*.

His first novel was *An Druma Mór*, a story of the rivalry between two pipe bands in a Donegal village. An Gúm, the Government Publishing Company, refused to publish the book on the grounds that the central character was readily identifiable and this might lead to a libel action. *An Druma Mór* was finally published in 1969. His collection of short stories, *An Grádh agus an Ghruaim* (1929) established him as a significant figure in Irish writing. Other well-known works were *Eoghan Ruadh O'Neill, Pádraig O'Conaire agus Aistí Eile,* and *Dochartach Dhuibhlionna*. His last works in 1935 were an autobiographical novel, *Mo Bhealach Féin*, and *Dá mbíodh Ruball ar an éan*, which ended with the words,

> Thráigh an tobar ins an tsamhradh 1935. Ní scríobhfaidh mé níos mó. Rinne mé mo dhicheall agus is cuma liom.
> (The well dried in the summer of 1935. I shall write no more. I did my best and I don't care).

During his early writing career, Mac Grianna also worked as a translator for An Gúm, under a scheme to provide Irish translations of English classics. From 1928 to 1935 he translated eleven books including works by Joseph Conrad and Sir Walter Scott, about a million words in all. Although he railed against the bureaucracy of An Gúm, he needed the money, and when the translation scheme was largely abandoned at the change of Government in 1932, he found himself in poor financial circumstances.

In the 1940s and 1950s Seosamh moved from lodgings to lodgings in Dublin, in dire financial straits. He was reduced to living on whatever his friends could give him and showed all the signs of mental deterioration. Niall Ó Dónaill describes Mac

Grianna's time living in Lilyvale cottage, as 'go huaigneach', and other friends who visited him there noted that he was living in squalor and was almost totally uncommunicative. He was a well-known figure walking the roads around Dollymount and Raheny and was regarded as an eccentric loner. In 1958 he suddenly disappeared from Lilyvale and his friends feared for his safety, but were relieved to hear that he had made his way back on foot to Rannafast. His family there, unable to care for him, had him placed in St. Conall's Hospital in Letterkenny. Apart from the occasional excursion over the years, he remained in the care of the hospital until his death on 11 June 1990. His private life was also unfortunate in that both his wife and son died tragically, a few months apart, in 1959.

Awareness and appreciation of Mac Grianna's contribution to Irish writing revived in the 1960s when *An Druma Mór* was finally published, and *An Grádh agus an Ghruaim* was reprinted. In 1971 he won the American Butler Prize of £2,000 for a work of literature in Irish. Mac Grianna is buried in Annagry Churchyard, a short distance from his native Rannafast.

MARIE ELIZABETH HAYES

(1874–1908)

DOCTOR AND MISSIONARY

Marie Elizabeth Hayes, the eldest daughter of the Rev. Francis Hayes and his wife Annabella Willson, was born on 17 May 1874, in the Glebe House, Raheny. Her father was appointed Rector of Raheny Parish in 1873 by Sir Arthur Guinness, later Lord Ardilaun, and served the parish for over forty years. At Raheny in 1887, her mother, Annabella Hayes founded the Mothers' Union of Ireland, which was, and still is, a Christian organisation promoting the well being of families.

Marie, known as May to her family, was a pupil of Alexandra College and then decided to study for a medical degree. As Trinity College did not accept women students, she studied at the Catholic University School of Medicine, attached to the Royal University of Ireland, which later became the National University of Ireland. She was a resident student for some months in the Coombe Hospital, Dublin and spent six months in the Mater Hospital, Dublin, which was the only hospital that admitted women as residents. Marie was conferred with the MB BCh BAO degrees on 12 May 1904 and of the five women conferred, she was the only one who obtained an Upper Pass. She qualified in surgery, pathology and obstetrics. After graduation, Marie served some months as a locum in the Belfast Infirmary. In preparation for work in India, she attended the School of Tropical Medicine in London and also undertook special missionary training and the study of the Urdu language.

In 1905 Marie went to work for the Cambridge Mission to Delhi in India. St. Stephen's Hospital, the first hospital for woman and children in Delhi was opened in 1885 by a group

Marie Elizabeth Hayes.

Graduation Photo of Marie Elizabeth Hayes.
Courtesy of the National Library of Ireland. Ref. No. Ir 92 H 121.

of missionary women and in 1891 Dr. Jenny Muller became the first full time doctor to the hospital. When Marie came to India, besides St. Stephen's Hospital in Delhi, the mission had another two hospitals; one, 70 miles to the north in Karnal and another, about 50 miles to the south in Rewari. Initially Marie worked mainly in Delhi and Karnal but later was given sole control of the hospital in Rewari. The Delhi hospital grew and in December 1906 the foundation stone was laid for the new St. Stephen's Hospital at its present site at Tis Hazari, in Old Delhi.

On New Year's Eve 1907 Marie travelled from Rewari to Delhi for a special celebration at St. Stephen's Community. Unexpectedly the following day, she became ill with pneumonia and died shortly afterwards on 4 January 1908, aged only 33 years. Her funeral service was held early the following morning in St. Stephen's Church, followed by burial in the Indian Christian Cemetery.

Glebe House (Raheny Rectory) where Marie Hayes was born in 1874.
Raheny Heritage Society.

The news of her death was sent immediately by telegram to her parents in Raheny. Her memorial service was held in All Saints' Church, Raheny, on 6 January 1908, the Feast of the Epiphany. It was conducted by a friend of her father, Rev. Precentor Hogan, and her cousin, Rev. Arthur Barton. The theme of the service was the 'Vision of God',

> She fell asleep her feet in Duty's path
> Her eyes uplifted to the guiding Star
> That led her Eastward.

Marie Hayes left a deep impression, particularly on her patients and colleagues in India, as well as her many friends and relatives in Dublin. Immediately after her death a Memorial Fund was set up in Dublin, chaired by the Church of Ireland Archbishop of Dublin, with many prominent Dublin people listed on the General Committee. Contributions to the fund came from friends and colleagues in Dublin, England and India. It was decided that the fund would be used for building a ward in the new St. Stephen's Hospital in Delhi to be named 'The Marie Hayes Ward'. In the hospital chapel a small memorial brass was also erected and a prayer-desk in the chapel bears an inscription in Urdu character, which translates as follows:

> For the service of God in prayer and in memory of Dr. Marie Hayes and what work she did. Placed here by nurses of Delhi, Karnal and Rewari. Year of Jesus, 1908.

The memorial in her home village took the form of a Celtic Cross and a pump erected on a rockery at the junction of Main Street and Watermill Road. Over the years it became the focal point for villagers to meet and chat. A few months after Marie's death, her parents travelled to India to visit all the places where she had worked. Her mother, Annabella Hayes kept all Marie's letters and after her death, she edited them and had them published. In the introduction to the book, Marie was described by the Rev. S. S. Allnuth, Head of the Cambridge Delhi Mission, as 'one of the choicest spirits with whom it has been my privilege to be associated during my 28

Marie Hayes Cross on its original site at the junction of Main Street
and Watermill Road in the 1940s.
ITA Collection, Courtesy of the Dublin City Library and Archive.

years of services'. Dr. Jenny Muller, first medical director of St. Stephen's Hospital, described Marie as 'an especially good surgeon; but keen as she was about her profession, the special work she was out here to do for the Lord and Master ever held a prominent place in her words and actions.'

The Marie Hayes Cross in Raheny was moved, due to road widening, in 1969 initially to the grounds of All Saints' Church, and then to the grassy area at the junction of Howth Road and Watermill Road. It was finally relocated in 2000 on a new plinth at the paved area beside St. Assam's Church and graveyard in the centre of the village. The inscription on the front of the Cross reads:

Marie Elizabeth Hayes
Doctor and Missionary,
Heal the sick
Say unto them
The Kingdom
of God is
Come unto You.

Marie Hayes Cross re-located on new plinth in 2000 beside the old St. Assam's Church and graveyard in the centre of Raheny Village. *J. Sharkey.*

Monsignor William J.

Fitzpatrick

(1893–1972)

PARISH PRIEST

William Joseph Fitzpatrick was appointed Parish Priest of Coolock in 1950, then Parish Priest of Killester/Raheny in 1955 and finally Parish Priest of Raheny in 1966 when it became a separate parish.

William was born in 1893 in Deerpark, Mountrath, Co. Laois of a farming family. He was educated at the Patrician Brothers' School, Mountrath, then at St. Kieran's College, Kilkenny and finished his secondary education at Rockwell College, Co. Tipperary. During these years he acquired a great love of Gaelic games and athletics.

In 1911 he began his studies for the priesthood at Clonliffe College, Dublin and took a First Class Honours Degree in Greek and Latin at University College, Dublin. He went to Rome in 1915 to continue his studies, obtaining a Degree of Doctor of Divinity in 1919. That same year he was ordained in the Basilica of St. John Lateran in Rome.

He returned to Dublin and worked firstly in the parish of Terenure and as Chaplain to the Presentation Sisters in Terenure. He was transferred to the Chaplaincy of the Little Sisters of the Assumption in Dun Laoghaire and later as Chaplain to the Ladies' Retirement Home on Portland Row, run by the Sisters of the Poor Servants of the Mother of God. During his time at Portland Row, he was assigned the task by the archbishop to translate into Latin from the English, for the purpose of sending to Rome, 'The Evidence of the Cause of the Irish Martyrs'.

Monsignor William Joseph Fitzpatrick, PP Raheny.
Raheny Heritage Society.

In 1926 he was appointed Curate at Fairview Parish. There, he took a keen interest in the sporting activities of the boys' school run by the Christian Brothers at Marino, and over the following years he helped coach the football and hurling teams in the Primary Schools' League. This area of the city was rapidly expanding with the building of the new Marino houses and new schools on Griffith Avenue. The schools were named St. Vincent de Paul and were also run by the Christian Brothers. Dr. Fitzpatrick was concerned about the lack of organised recreational facilities for the increasing number of boys in the parishes of Fairview and Marino. Following a conversation between Dr. Fitzpatrick and Brother Ernest Fizgerald, a teacher in O'Connell School, North Richmond Street, on this subject, they established the St. Vincent's Hurling and Football Club in 1931.

Over the following decades the club became synonymous with success at all levels and contributed significantly to the success of Dublin county teams in hurling and football. In 1953 the club provided fourteen of the Dublin team that brought home the National League title to Dublin. St.Vincent's became one of the foremost GAA Clubs in the country, and many of its players became household names in the GAA world; Kevin Heffernan and Tony Hanahoe to name but two. Dr. Fitzpatrick became a Life President of the Club. On the occasion of the Silver Jubilee of the club in 1956, at a dinner held in the Gresham Hotel, a gold and silver chalice was presented to Dr. Fitzpatrick, which was made by smelting down all the medals won by players of the club over the past 25 years. It was a fitting tribute to the co-founder of the Club, which Dr. Fitzpatrick greatly appreciated. This chalice is still used today in the present Catholic Church in Raheny.

The St. Vincent's Club did not have a permanent ground until 1959 when they acquired the former pony trotting ground, called 'The Oval', on Raheny Road. This site is now covered by the Ashcroft houses. The Oval served the club for many years, but in 1981 the club returned to its roots in Marino to a site near the St. Vincent de Paul National Schools.

Fitzpatrick Chalice.
Raheny Heritage Society.

Dr. Fitzpatrick was transferred in 1949 to the parish of Coolock which then included the parishes of Killester and Raheny within its boundary. The following year he was appointed Parish Priest of Coolock. He was an outstanding administrator with a natural flair for organisation and was instrumental in

Front cover of *The Acorn* magazine.

the establishment of several new parishes in north Dublin over the years. He became Parish Priest of the separate parish of Killester and Raheny in 1955 and he settled in Raheny, which was expanding with massive housing developments. He oversaw the building of the Catholic Church, Our Lady, Mother of Divine Grace in Raheny in 1962 and became Parish Priest of Raheny when it became a separate parish in 1966. He was also responsible for the building of primary and secondary schools in Raheny and Edenmore. He was made a Vicar General of the Archdiocese in 1960 and shortly afterwards chosen as a Canon of the Metropolitan Chapter. He was created a Domestic Prelate by Rome with the title of Monsignor by 1967.

Monsignor Fitzpatrick started the magazine, *The Acorn,* for the Killester/Raheny parish in 1960 for which he researched and wrote many articles on the local history of the area. These articles are greatly used by present day students, both young and old. He died on 5 January 1972 and is buried in the grounds of the Church of Our Lady, Mother of Divine Grace.

Senator James Dunne

(1921-1972)

Trade Unionist

Jimmy Dunne was a resident of St. Anne's Estate, Raheny from 1954 until his death in 1972. He was born and reared in the Pearse Street-South Quays area of Dublin City and was educated at St. Andrew's National School. On leaving school he worked as a general labourer, then joined the National Army and served throughout the Emergency, which was the name given to the period of the Second World War in Ireland. After the war, during periods of unemployment, he experienced the awakening of a social conscience, which was to mould and motivate him throughout his working life, as he showed his unbending commitment to improving the lot of the general worker. An admirer of James Connolly, he believed that all Irish people should have the chance to share equitably in the resources of the nation.

Jimmy Dunne worked for the Dublin Gas Company and then the Electricity Supply Board, where he was a shop steward. As a member of the Marine Port and General Workers Union (MPGWU) he was appointed Branch Secretary in 1953 and General Secretary in 1957. From 1960 he was also a member of the executive of the Irish Congress of Trade Unions (ICTU). He was Vice-President of Congress during 1967-68 and President for 1968-69. Some of the most difficult and fateful disputes in the history of the State arose during his term as President. His role during the maintenance workers' strike brought him further into national prominence, when his defence of Congress policy was vigorous and forthright. He spoke of his hurt at the senseless and mostly unnecessary damage done to MPGWU and affiliated organisations by the selfishness of small groups of union members, which made thousands of other workers unemployed.

Senator James Dunne.
Raheny Heritage Society.

He represented ICTU at meetings and conferences abroad. Jimmy was a member of the Dublin Port and Docks Board, the Irish National Productivity Committee, the Dublin Institute of Adult Education and the Dublin Itinerants' Settlement Committee. He participated in the setting up of adult education facilities in the city and attended extra mural courses at UCD and the College of Industrial Relations. He held diplomas in Social Science and Economic Studies.

At the general election in 1969, on the nomination of Congress, Jimmy was elected to the Labour Panel of Seanad Éireann. Addressing a Fianna Fáil seminar in Barley Cove Hotel, Cork in February 1970, he pointed out that, while strikes should not be a primary objective of trade unions, they represented a failure on the part of employers and the community to recognise and to contribute to the legitimate demands of workers. His contributions both in the Seanad and outside were outstanding for their sincerity and courage. His many speeches included the following observations:

> While man does not live by bread alone, he dies without it. (1970)

> The curse of our country is division, and almost every worthwhile effort of our people has foundered on the rock of disunity. (1972)

Senator Dunne participated actively in the Seanad during his period of service, which was sadly cut short by a serious and protracted illness. He died at St. Joseph's Nursing Home, Raheny on 23 February 1972, aged 51, leaving a wife and ten children. He is buried in Balgriffin Cemetery. Among the many tributes paid to Senator Dunne, Mr. Frank Ellis, President of the MPGWU and a close friend, said he 'would miss him for his sound judgment, ripe wisdom and strength of character'. Other tributes came from Labour leader, Mr. Brendan Corish, and the Dublin Port and Docks Board. The weekly meeting of the Parliamentary Labour Party was adjourned as a mark of respect. A spokesman for the Federated Union of Employers (FUE) spoke of Senator Dunne's ability and integrity as a trade union negotiator.

In his final speech as President of Congress, Jimmy Dunne said his philosophy was a very simple one:

> God, in whom I believe, never meant his creatures to suffer want, hunger or loneliness, and I will subscribe to any form of society in which these human-inflicted evils disappear.

BIBLIOGRAPHY

SAMUEL DICK

Appleyard, Douglas. S, *In and Out of School: over two centuries of Coolock and Raheny Schools*, (Dublin 1989).
Dublin Historical Record, V. 3, No. 2. 'The Ouzel Galley' by G.A. Little.
Hall, F.G., *History of the Bank of Ireland*, (Dublin, 1949).
Dublin Directories, various issues from 1762 to 1795.

JOHN D'ARCY

Barnard, Alfred, *The Noted Breweries of Great Britain and Ireland, Vol. 2.*, (UK 1889).
Dublin Historical Record, Vol. 16, 1960-61.
Freeman's Journal, 10 & 22 September 1823; 2 March 1864.
The Acorn, July/August 1963.

JANE BARLOW

Tynan, Katharine, *Memories,* (London, 1924).
Hogan, Robert, (Ed.), *Dictionary of Irish Literature,* (Dublin, 1980).
Welch, Robert, (Ed.), *The Oxford Companion to Irish Literature,* (Oxford, 2001).
The Acorn, September/October 1961; March/April 1962.
The Times, 21 April 1917.
Irish Independent, 18 April 1917.

FRANK GALLAGHER

Boylan, Henry, *A Dictionary of Irish Biography,* (Dublin, 1998).
Hogan, David, *The Four Glorious Years*, (Dublin, 1953).
McRedmond, Louis, *Modern Irish Lives*, (Dublin, 1996).
The Irish Press, 5 September 1931; 5 September 1981.
The Irish Times, 16 & 17 July 1962.
Conversations with Ann Gallagher, daughter.

JOHN SWEETMAN

Madden, Richard Robert, *The United Irishmen, their lives and times*, 3rd Series, (Dublin, 1846); *The United Irishmen, their lives and times,* (Newly edited with notes, bibliography and index by Vincent Fleming O'Reilly, New York, 1916).
The Acorn, July/August 1962; March/April, 1963.
Irish Architectural Archive, Biographical Index of Irish Architects (database by Ann Martha Rowan, 2007).
Donnelly, Rev. N., D.D., *Short Histories of Dublin Parishes, Part XII, Pro-Cathedral, Marlborough Street.* Carraig Chapbooks (no date)
Father Phelim, ODC, *St. Teresa's Church, Clarendon Street.* (no date)
Irish excavations reports, Dublin 1999-2000, database, www.excavations.ie

WILLIAM SWEETMAN

The Acorn, September/October 1962; May/June 1963.
Appleyard, Douglas. S, *In and Out of School: over two centuries of Coolock and Raheny Schools,* (Dublin 1989).
Sweetman family wills, National Archives.
Registry of Deeds, various years.
Faulkener's Journal, February 1758.
Freeman's Journal, various issues.
Dublin Directories, 1820-1862.

THOMAS MICHAEL GRESHAM

O'Connor, Ulick, *The Gresham Hotel 1865 – 1965,* (Cork, 1965).
The Irish Builder, various years.
Registry of Deeds, various years.
The Freeman's Journal, 9 May 1871.
Garrett, Arthur, *Through Countless Ages: The story of the church and parish of All Saints' Raheny* (Dublin 1989).
Joyce, St. John Weston, *The Neighbourhood of Dublin,* (Dublin, 1912, Reprinted 1994).
Thom's Directories, 1844-1872.

STEPHEN LUCIUS GWYNN

Gwynn, Stephen, *For Second Reading,* (Dublin 1918).
Legg, L.G. Wickham & E.T. Williams (Eds.), *The Dictionary of National Biography,1941-1950,* (Oxford University Press, 1959).
The Irish Times, 12 June 1950.
Irish Press, 12 June 1950.
The Times, 12 June 1950.
The Acorn, March/April 1961, 'Raheny Fifty Years Ago' by Denis Gwynn.
Burke's Irish Family Records, (London, 1976).

George Papworth

Irish Architectural Archive, Biographical Index of Irish Architects (database by Ann Martha Rowan, 2007).
Matthew, H.C. G. & Brian Harrison (Eds.), *Oxford Dictionary of National Biography*, (Oxford University Press, 2004).
The Builder, 31 March 1855.
Ball, Francis Elrington, *Howth and its Owners: A History of Co. Dublin*, Vol. 5, (Dublin, 1917, Reprinted 1979).
D'Alton, John, *The History of the County of Dublin*, (Dublin, 1838, Reprinted Cork 1976).
Thom's Directories, various years.

William Dargan

Boylan, Henry, *Dictionary of National Biography*, (Dublin, 1998).
Dublin Historical Record, various issues.
Freeman's Journal, various issues.
The Times, various issues.
Thom's Directories, 1849 – 1860.

Richard Kelly

The Acorn, March/April & September/October 1963; January/February 1964.
Papers of Rector Paul Cullen and Rector Tobias Kirby, Archives of the Pontifical Irish College, Rome; KIR/1847, No. 586; 1852, No. 1015 & 1055; CUL/ No. 1893.
Correspondence with Irish Architectural Archives, re Manor House, April 2006.
Freeman's Journal, various years.
The Times, various years.
Registry of Deeds, 1848, Book 12, No. 27.
Liverpool Mercury, 30 October 1829.
Irish Builder, June 1869.
Thom's Directories, various years.

Benjamin Lee Guinness & Arthur Edward Guinness.

Ussher Sharkey, Joan, *St. Anne's: the story of a Guinness Estate*, (Dublin, 2002).

Lynch, Patrick & John Vaizey, *Guinness's Brewery in the Irish Economy*, 1759-1876, (Cambridge, 1960).

Malins, Edward & Patrick Bowe, *Irish Gardens and Demesnes since 1830*, (London, 1980).

Garrett, Arthur, *Through Countless Ages: the story of the Church and Parish of All Saints' Raheny*, (Dublin 1989).

Patrick Boland, Snr. & Jnr.

History of the Boland family with memories of Patrick Boland, written by his son, John Pius Boland after 1928. (Private record, held by Anne O'Rourke.)

Ussher Sharkey, Joan, *St. Anne's: the story of a Guinness Estate*, (Dublin, 2002).

Boland, Bridget, *At My Mother's Knee*, (London, 1978).

UCD Graduates Magazine, 1984, 'John Pius Boland: Scholar-Athlete-Statesman and the Establishment of the National University of Ireland' by Cyril White.

Freeman's Journal, 16 December 1871.

Henry Chichester Hart

Mollan, Davis & Finucan, (Eds.), *More People and Places in Irish Science and Technology*, (RIA, Dublin, 1990); *Irish Innovators in Science and Technology*, (RIA, Dublin, 2002).

Nugent, Frank, *Seek the Frozen Lands: Irish Polar Explorers 1740-1922*, (Cork, 2003).

Freeman's Journal, various years.

George Derwent Thomson

Journal of Kerry Archaeological & Historical Society. No. 13 1980, p. 149-172, 'Seoirse Mac Tomáis – George Derwent Thomson', by Seán Ó Lúing.

O'Sullivan, Maurice, *Twenty Years A-Growing*, translated by Moya Llewelyn Davies and George Thomson; foreword by E. M. Forster, (London, 1933).

Ó Súileabháin Muiris, *Fiche Blian ag Fás*, (Dublin, 1933).

The Irish Times, 11 February 1987.

The Times, 7 February 1987.

The Acorn, January/February 1962.

Seosamh Mac Grianna

Ó Muirí, Pól, *A Flight from Shadow: the life and work of Seosamh Mac Grianna*, (Belfast 1999).

Cómhar, January 1988, 'Seosamh Mac Grianna', by Niall O Dónaill,

BBC Northern Ireland, documentary film, 'Dá mbíodh Ruball ar an Éan,' 1991.

The Irish Times, 13 June 1990.

Marie Elizabeth Hayes

Hayes, Annabella, (Ed.), *At Work: letters of Marie Elizabeth Hayes, M.B. Missionary Doctor, Delhi, 1905-8*, (London, 1909).

Crofton, Denis Hayes, *The Children of Edmonstown Park: memoirs of an Irish family*, (Peterhead, Scotland, 1980).

Church of Ireland Gazette, various issues.

The Irish Times, various issues.

Hartford, D.M., *Among the Gaiters*, (Portlaw, Waterford, Volturna Press, 1970).

St. Stephen's Hospital Brochures and website> www.ststephenshospital.org

Monsignor William J. Fitzpatrick

Donnelly, Paddy, *Cumann Iomáine agus Peile, Naomh Uinsionn, 1931–1981,* (no date).
Correspondence with Dublin Diocesan Archives.
Irish Catholic Directories, various years.
St. Vincent's GAA website> www.stvincentgaa.ie

Senator James Dunne

Irish Congress of Trade Unions' reports, 1968, 1969, 1970.
Nevin, Donal, (Ed.), *Trade Union Century,* (Cork, Dublin, 1994).
Seanad Éireann, Vol. 72, 23 February 1972.
Irish Times, 24 & 25 February 1972.
Sunday Independent, various issues in 1967 & 1969 and 1 March 1970.
Conversations with Mrs. Mary Carroll (daughter).

INDEX

HOUSES

Ashford Estate 49,56
Ballyhoy 6,9,10
Bedford Lodge 48
Belvidere House 61
Bettyville Cottage 32
Bettyville House 40
Cottage, The 6,10,9
Crescent Cottages 3,5,22,56
Dick's Charity School 3,5,4
Edenmore House 1
Fox Hall 17,21
Fox House 17,25,19,27
Furry Park House 66,68
Garda Retirement Home 13
Glebe House, Raheny (Rectory) 74,76
Glenalla 65
Glenvar 63
Hinchogue 32
Kenure House, Rush 35
Kilbarrack House 5
Lilyvale 70,73
Manor House 40,41,43,45
Maryville House 36,38,39,54
Middleton Park House 35
Raheny House 6,9,10,13,15,20,22,23,24
Raheny Park 17,25,27,28,30,61
Rathmore 22,23,24
St. Anne's 46,48,49,50,52,54,56
St. Valerie, Bray 12
Stillorgan Park 46
Sybil Hill 36,54
Thornhill 46
Village House, the 3
Violet Hill 1,3
Watermill Cottage 66,68
Watermill House 58,59,61
Winton House 61

PEOPLE

Allnuth, Rev. S.S. 77
Ardilaun, Lady 3,57
Ardilaun, Lord (see Arthur Edward Guinness)
Ashlin, George Coppinger 54,56
Atkinson, Mary Anne 19
Ball, Francis E. 32
Bantry, William, 3rd Earl of 52
Barlow, Jane 10,11,12,13
Barlow, Rev. James William 10
Barton, Rev. Arthur 77
Beauman, William 25
Boland, Bridget 62
Boland, Elizabeth 59,61
Boland, John Pius 62
Boland, Mary 61,62
Boland, Patrick, Jnr. 58, 61,62
Boland, Patrick, Snr. 58,59,61
Bond, Oliver 20
Brennan, Bob 15
Browne, Dr. Noel 16
Byrne, Edward 6
Byrne, John Dominic 6
Casement, Roger 30
Cheshire, Mary 65
Childers, Erskine 15
Christopher 'the blind lord of Howth' 32
Connolly, James 86
Conrad, Joseph 72
Corish, Brendan 88
Cosgrave, Jane 22
Crowley, Mrs. Honor 62
Cullen, Dr. 40,41,43
D'Alton, John 32
D'Arcy, Arthur 8
D'Arcy, Eliza 6
D'Arcy, Jane 6
D'Arcy, John 6,7,8,9
D'Arcy, Mary 6
D'Arcy, Matthew 6
D'Arcy, Matthew Peter 6
Dargan, William 36,37,38,39
Davies, Margaret 32

General Topics